FOLLOW YOUR BLISS!

A PRACTICAL, SOUL-CENTERED GUIDE TO JOB HUNTING
AND CAREER-LIFE PLANNING

HALEY FOX

iUniverse

FOLLOW YOUR BLISS!
A PRACTICAL, SOUL-CENTERED GUIDE TO JOB HUNTING AND CAREER-LIFE PLANNING

iUniverse books may be ordered through booksellers or by contacting:

iUniverse
1663 Liberty Drive
Bloomington, IN 47403
www.iuniverse.com
1-800-Authors (1-800-288-4677)

Because of the dynamic nature of the Internet, any web addresses or links contained in this book may have changed since publication and may no longer be valid. The views expressed in this work are solely those of the author and do not necessarily reflect the views of the publisher, and the publisher hereby disclaims any responsibility for them.

Any people depicted in stock imagery provided by Getty Images are models,
and such images are being used for illustrative purposes only.
Certain stock imagery © Getty Images.

ISBN: 978-1-5320-9140-7 (sc)
ISBN: 978-1-5320-9141-4 (e)

Library of Congress Control Number: 2019921176

Print information available on the last page.

iUniverse rev. date: 01/17/2020

TABLE OF CONTENTS

FOREWORD TO THE SECOND EDITION

I first met Haley Fox in the late 1970s in Portland, Oregon. I was a Vietnam veteran who had been injured in the war. At that time, I was as working as a job developer for disabled veterans, helping to establish the beginnings of what would eventually become the disability civil rights movement, which twenty years later (in 1990) resulted in the passage of the Americans with Disabilities Act.

Haley was coordinating a national program advocating for the employment of persons with epilepsy. We met at a free community training I was conducting for persons with disabilities on job finding and the role employment can have on increasing the quality of life for those who find the right job.

We have kept in touch over the years, and I have been both pleased and enlightened with the way that she has stayed the course. Her studies concerning the relationship between work and life satisfaction have redefined the way many of her peers in the employment field now view work. They have come to see a job as more than just a way to achieve the goal of making a living, but also as a way to enhance the quality and meaning of our lives.

I have been fortunate enough to be involved with work that has allowed me to grow, develop, and follow my bliss. While I know that everyone will not achieve this, I nonetheless remain convinced that everyone deserves it.

I meet people every day. One of the questions I am most often asked is, "What do you do?" While this is an employment question, it is potentially a metaphysical question as well. When I am asked that question, I simply answer, "About what?" The reaction I see in their faces is precious. It is more than just a question that strangers ask us. It is also a question we should ask ourselves. The answer can be the bridge that connects your bliss to your job.

I encourage you not to just take my word for it. I would like to share with you some thoughts of others who have influenced me.

This quote is commonly attributed to Albert Einstein: "Everybody is a genius. But if you judge a fish by its ability to climb a tree, it will live its whole life believing that it is stupid." The question many of us ask when we read this quote is, "What is my genius?" The book *Follow Your Bliss!* does so much more than just ask that. It challenges each of us to take the next positive step in our journey. It encourages us to escape the dense vocational forest that so many of us find ourselves in. It helps to light our path to leave the trees and to search for our lake. Once in that lake, we will not have the time to ask what our genius is. We will be too busy blissfully swimming to give it even a second thought.

Many of us look to find a job that will finally bring us bliss. But does a job really bring bliss to us, or do we bring our bliss to our jobs? This book explores in a very fundamental way whether work and its environment "gives us bliss" or whether work provides us with an environment that allows the bliss that is already in us and constantly developing to thrive and amalgamate with our work to create a whole that is far greater than the sum of its parts.

In order to realize that we should search for our lake, we first must discover that we want to swim. That is why this book guides us to first identify what our bliss is and then find the work environment where it can thrive.

In 2007, I was asked to give a talk for a free children's hospital in Dallas. The audience was made up of parents of the children, medical staff, and volunteers. This is what I said: "The shortest distance between where these children are now and where they want to be is a road that is illuminated by their own dreams. Not the dreams that we have for them. No matter how much we know or how much we love them."

Your road is illuminated by your own dreams. Don't change your dreams to fit your situation; change your situation to fit your dreams. This book is a blueprint for doing just that.

Here are two similar quotes that have had a significant impact on my view of the role of employment and its relationship to our personal satisfaction.

"Many people die with their music still in them. Why is this so? Too often it is because they are always getting ready to live. Before they know it, time runs out" (Oliver Wendell Holmes Sr.).

"Most men lead lives of quiet desperation and go to the grave with their song still in them" (Henry David Thoreau).

When I first read the book *Follow Your Bliss!*, I realized that it was an affirmation that none of us should ever go to our graves with our music still inside us or our songs unsung. We all have music. This book does more than instruct us to find that music; it helps us to believe our music is worthwhile, and having found our music, this book helps us find a work environment where our music can be played by us and appreciated by all who hear it.

In my early days of job developing for disabled veterans, there were three elements that I believed were necessary for my job satisfaction.

1. Belong: I must find a work environment where I feel I belong. Where I am comfortable, respected, and valued.

2. Believe: I need a work environment where I believe that what I am doing is more than just the sum of its parts—that I am accomplishing something that has a greater purpose than the mundane, day-to-day parts of my job. That my contribution makes a difference to support something greater than just myself. I never wished to be large. I wished to be a part of something larger than myself.

3. Become: Life is more than a job. I am always learning, evolving, and becoming more than I was the day before. My ideal job not only helps me to make a difference to others but also to make a difference to myself.

I believe this book will help you find and follow your bliss. Not just because you can do it. Haley Fox wrote it for a far more important reason than that. She wrote it because you are worth it.

Dr. Richard Pimentel
April 15, 2019

PREFACE

I'll do anything. I don't care about a career. I just need a job.
—Anonymous

Life is too short to be spent at a job that holds no personal value—or, in the worst-case scenario, a job that evokes apathy, misery, or contempt. And yet, many of us feel painfully insecure about our abilities to find meaning and satisfaction in work.

On the other hand, let me introduce you to Joe the Conductor. Around the time I wrote the first edition of this book, I often spoke about Joe in workshops I conducted around Massachusetts. I never knew Joe's real name, but I knew his presence well. He rode the commuter rail between Boston and Fitchburg, and he lived and breathed his job so naturally, with such zest and pride, that it was nearly impossible to imagine him in any other role. I could tell by the proud way he sauntered through the aisles and bellowed out his stops that he loved his job. The most amazing thing was, the moment I began to describe Joe during my workshops, at least one or two people in the room who had ridden the rail knew exactly of whom I spoke.

Joe the Conductor was one of those fortunate individuals who had found a way to follow his bliss, to borrow a phrase from the late Joseph Campbell. I have grown fond of the term *bliss*. Webster defines *bliss* as "perfect happiness" and "heavenly joy," which implies a divine connection. The word is originally derived from the Greek *bhlei,* meaning "to shine." For me, bliss arrives in grace-filled moments when I am *me* most completely; when I lose track of time in the midst of a creative endeavor; when a tragedy calls forth strengths I didn't know I had; when a stunning sunset prompts me to pause and consider my place in the universe. Bliss even accompanies rare moments when I let down my guard and face my inadequacies.

In the pages to follow, I hope to make the path to bliss more available to you and to advance the following notions.

- Like everyone, you deserve more than "just a job"; you deserve bliss.
- You have the potential to achieve bliss.
- You have an obligation to make use of the gifts and talents that uniquely equip you for soul-nourishing work—and, incidentally, lead to bliss.

It may seem easy to acknowledge that everyone deserves joy and satisfaction in work. Still, many people behave as though they do not deserve it. The phenomenon seems to have sprouted in part from puritanical roots that framed work as drudgery to be performed with perseverance and humility, but not necessarily with enjoyment—or, heaven forbid, with passion.

The attitude of work as drudgery reflects in the way we use language to describe work. We make clear distinctions between work and play. And those who dare to admit, "I love this job—I can't believe they pay me to do this!" can meet with disapproval, jealousy, or derision. Some may feel inclined to apologize for enjoying their work.

When people view joy and passion in work as a luxury—or worse, as mutually exclusive terms—we should not be surprised that they approach a job search with reluctance or dread and low expectations. Paradoxically, this attitude works against the job seeker. Rather than face greater numbers of opportunities—which some assume an "I'll take anything" approach will yield—we more often find ourselves immobilized, rudderless, and ill equipped to inspire the help and involvement of others. Success, as it turns out, characteristically eludes those who lack the focus and direction of a *Follow Your Bliss!* approach.

I like to tell people that joy in life and work arises as a by-product of being in alignment with a deeper purpose that is every bit as connected with the world and what the world needs from you as it is with your own personal passion. In fact, passion originates in that deeper place. That is precisely what guides the quest for bliss.

In short, *Follow Your Bliss!* supports the search for purposeful, meaningful, satisfying work that meets real needs in the world, offering thought-provoking exercises, creative activities, and words of encouragement. It is best studied and worked on within a small group or at least with a partner. I have found that dialogue among people inspires imaginative ideas and support and makes the work richer. The ideal arrangement, in my view, is for individuals or groups to work in partnership with an art therapist or an expressive arts therapist or coach with special training in the use and interpretation of artistic as well as verbal expressions.

Following from the notion that the key to happiness in work is rooted in a commitment to following bliss, this workbook strives to show you how. I will guide you to reflect upon clues tucked into your past experience and to engage in guided imagery and other excursions into the imaginal realm designed to get you in touch with your bliss. I will offer further inspiration to follow bliss in stories, writing prompts, and an array of art-based exercises. Practical approaches to the nuts and bolts of career-life planning are also included here, from how to prepare a professional portfolio to locating job leads and interviewing for positions that promise the best possible fit. A complete list of exercises can be found at the end of this book.

ACKNOWLEDGMENTS

This book worked on me for many years, nurtured by the support and encouragement I received from mentors and friends who have urged me to follow my own bliss. I published the first edition in 2000, as a capstone to years of working in the field of career-life planning, first as program director for the Epilepsy Foundation of America's Training and Placement Service (TAPS) and later through my own private practice, CareerLife Visions. Along the way, these influential people (in consecutive order) have been most impactful in shaping the ideas and practices discussed in this book: Kimberly Gronewald Hall, Bob Goheen, Pat Hillquist, Dr. Mary J. Nicholas, Mary Benson, Michael Cosky, Catherine Hayes, Bernie Wolfard, Richard Pimentel (who wrote the foreword to this second edition), Bill Murphy, Dan Shapiro, Meredith Harron, Paolo Knill, Shaun McNiff (who wrote the foreword to the first edition), Joan Hanley (a.k.a. Hari Kirin), Elizabeth David, Eileen Feldman, Kit Jenkins, Sara Tsutsumi, and all those with whom I sang and played at the St. Michael Choir in Prior Lake, Minnesota—especially Jean Thompson. A smile warms my face as I think of each of you, one by one. How great the impact the lot of you have had upon my creative life!

That was many years ago, and I am blessed to remain in close contact with many of you. Your good company has been joined by a few notable and inspiring others, namely, Tina Thomas, Don Frick, Simon Jay, Chris Noble, and especially Dave Perez. I feel your wind beneath my wings every day. Of course, I owe a considerable debt of gratitude to my clients, my students, and my supervisees seeking professional credentialing. You make me a better person through the work that I do.

To my children, Genevieve, Sam, Jackie, and David: you make me proud, and my greatest wish for you is that you find, follow, and stay true to your bliss for the remainder of your days.

Haley Fox
April 18, 2019

TABLE OF EXERCISES

TABLE OF FIGURES

REIMAGINING THE GAME

Everything we know and feel
and every statement we make
[is] fantasy-based; that is,
[everything] derives from psychic images.
—James Hillman

The quest upon which we are about to embark, more than anything else, requires generous measures of imagination and courage. Each of these qualities deserves further mention here.

The Power of Imagination

Let me begin by sharing a basic governing principle: the way we imagine our lives has far more power than any *consensual* or *actual* reality.

It is the way we imagine ourselves and the world around us—not any fantasies we have about an "objective, out-there" reality—that plays the dominant role in dictating how we behave in the world. The eating disorder anorexia nervosa provides a striking and sobering example. Our vision of a beautiful, young woman wasting away by deliberately starving herself simply does not match the girl's own vision of a grossly overweight person buried under heavy folds of skin

> *The way we imagine our lives has far more power than any consensual or actual reality.*

and fat. For her, refusing to eat is not as simple as a cry for attention; it actually arises from an altered way of imagining reality. The girl behaves in full accordance with her perceived reality.

An example more pertinent to the career search can be found in a story from writer and philosopher Sam Keen (best known for his 1991 book *Fire in the Belly: On Being a Man*). In an interview with Bill Moyers (*Your Mythic Journey*, 1991), Dr. Keen tells of his high-achiever brother who had developed a reputation in the family for superior mechanical ability. Young Sam saw himself, in comparison, as someone who could never quite measure up. As an adult, he took an achievement test in the hopes of getting guidance in choosing a career. When the guidance counselor presented him with his results, he was not surprised to hear that his scores fell "in the fifth percentile."

"That sounds about right." Sam nodded. "So, 95 percent of the people tested scored better than I did."

"No, no," replied the counselor. "You're in the top 5 percent. Ninety-five percent scored lower than you."

"No, that's my brother," Sam answered.

From an early age, Sam had imagined that he lacked mechanical ability. He mentally allowed his brother to fully inhabit that terrain, and his imagination strongly influenced his behavior.

The power of imagination can erect obstacles if we allow it, but it can also be a great gift. If you give yourself permission to imagine yourself doing what you love, doing it well, and enjoying success, then you come that much closer to actually being there. This is the law of attraction, and it is no trick. It is a legitimate tool for cultivating a resource far more powerful than—and just as real as—consensual reality.

The law of attraction found a foothold in popular consciousness with the publication of *The Secret* by Rhonda Byrne (2006). The invitation to "create your own reality" inspired many and quite likely frustrated many as well. Counselors and professional life coaches from all over the globe incorporated law of attraction strategies into their practices. Certain people insist they have killed cancers by imagining them gone—not as a fleeting imagining, but repeatedly, with faith and with great detail (Siegel 1986). How much more difficult can it be to land yourself in a career for which you are superbly suited?

Today, the new physics and, in particular, Robert Lanza's proposed "theory of everything," biocentrism (2009), offers increasing support for the notion that nothing exists outside of human perception—that consciousness has indeed preceded and continues to precede the unfolding of our material world (or worlds). Incidentally, Robert Lanza is no slouch; a medical doctor, he is widely considered to be one of the most important scientists in the world today.

I believe that most people miss the mark in one respect when attempting to apply the law of attraction to their career-life planning endeavors. The problem, as I see it, relates to how we define the *I* who sets out to imagine a goal.

Most of us think of *I* as what psychologists might call the ego. Ego is an interesting character. He generally imagines himself "the only one" (the masculine used arbitrarily here), certainly the one in charge. In fact, *many* characters populate consciousness: the "devil on your shoulder," your "better angels," the array of characters that enter your dreams, the human shadow you cannot bear to look at, the voice of a critical parent who arises to influence choice-making (even when the actual parent is deceased). Ego simply serves as the facilitator of all those characters and personas.

Jung conceptualized two selves: the small *s* self (ego) and the large *S* Self, described as a divine, spiritual center. *Self* in this context is a "higher" Self, and even if we conceptualize this Self to reside within us, it is nevertheless characterized by a quality of otherness. This Self goes by many names: God, Source, the universe, the ground of all being, the collective unconscious, inspiration, or, my personal favorite, the Giver of Art—and of bliss.

If we truly want to benefit from the law of attraction, we will find the most success when we ask ourselves not what ego desires but rather what our higher Self desires—or, better, what the universe requires of us. How can we best serve the world? What is the best use of the myriad talents and gifts with which we have been blessed? Source is ever eager to assist in achieving these ends.

On the other hand, if you decide (or imagine) that you have no hope of ever finding bliss— or more specifically in this context, of ever finding happiness in a job—guess what? This imagined intention becomes your reality. There is no hope of finding bliss, not because of any literal, objective, preexisting out-there reality but rather because of how you have imagined (and thereby created) your reality. Applying a thoroughly pragmatic attitude to this, if you imagine hopelessness, how can you put more than a half-hearted effort into a job search? By the same token, what prospective employer will want to hire someone with such a Debbie Downer attitude?

The phenomenon of the power of imagination holds true not only for individuals but also for the collective awareness of our culture. As a case in point, consumer confidence has a huge impact on our economy, and it is as simple as this: When we have confidence in the health of the economy, we spend, and in doing so we feed the economy. When we feed our economy, it grows. A weak economy can only be aided when consumer confidence is high and leads to increased spending. On the other hand, no amount of wealth stashed away will help an economy when its keeper lacks confidence in his or her own employability and/or in the capacity of the economy to meet the need for meaningful employment.

> *If we truly want to benefit from the law of attraction, we will find the most success when we ask ourselves not what our ego desires but rather what our higher Self desires—or, better, what the universe requires of us.*

At various times in history, the United States has been bathed in hopelessness and doom. The economy was thought to be bad. Those who imagined this as our social reality, not surprisingly, tended to receive just what they imagined.

We often imagine things to be worse than they actually are, and this tendency exacerbates situations by dictating behavior that simply continues to reinforce our mistaken beliefs. What is more, such pessimism can literally keep us from hearing good news. There is always good news to be had, for certain die-hards among us continue to approach life with optimism and continue to manifest good things in the world.

When I wrote the first edition of this book, I noted that the number of available jobs in the United States actually rose by over twenty million during what was viewed as a bad economy between 1970 and 1980 (Wegmann et al. 1989, 7). Another ten million jobs were added in 1986. Unemployment ran high for a time, only because of an increase in people seeking work, most notably a flood of baby boomers, immigrants, and women. This sudden, uneven growth put the mix of jobs in flux. As the economy grew stronger, the unemployment rate continued to decline.

Sadly, many people fail to adjust their expectations, even with improving economic conditions. Comprehending and adapting to monumental changes in the nature of work and the workforce—including creative ventures engaged by "free range humans" (Cantwell 2013) and "minimalists" (Fields and Nicodemus 2014)—can be understandably difficult to grasp and to engage.

A healthy imagination helps us to face change and new possibilities with greater ease, to recognize bliss when it beckons us, and to be more effective problem solvers. We can benefit greatly from spending time just increasing our comfort within the imaginal realm. Countless avenues to engage imagination exist: art-making, play, invention, and creative collaboration with others. Here's a simple game that you can do with a few friends.

Exercise 1: Point A to Point B

Designate a point A and point B in a large room or outdoors, roughly ten to twenty feet apart. Everyone lines up behind point A. Then, one at a time, each person moves from point A to point B in any way he or she wishes. The only rule is no one can move in a way that has already been used. Typically, people walk, run, hop, and skip—and then wonder what else to do. But as they exercise imagination, they come up with all kinds of ways to move (slither, sneak, cartwheel, crab walk, tango, dribble an imaginary basketball, ice-skate), sometimes in character (stumble as if intoxicated, do a sexy walk, try out a John Wayne saunter). Anyone who repeats another person's movement is out. The game ends when only one person remains.

Courage

A fertile and active imagination cannot propel a person on the path to soul-nourishing work without a generous measure of courage. There are certain to be obstacles on this path, moments of doubt and fear.

For the most part, fear cannot be avoided. Courage has been defined as the ability to feel the fear and do it anyway (Jeffers 1987). Courage means stretching past the safe boundaries of a daily routine and rising to meet the challenges that call you. This can be mighty scary. But as the saying goes, if you're never scared, then you can never know true courage.

Many need help to muster the courage and confidence required in the new economy, in which change happens rapidly and people must rely more than ever upon their own self-awareness, ingenuity, and skills at self-promotion. Few employers today can promise a lifetime of employment security in one place. While opportunities to follow bliss may be expanding, the courage to follow bliss can often be lacking. Sometimes the first step toward mustering courage is to ask for help—from a career counselor, a therapist, a professional résumé writer, or from a friend who believes in you. But taking the first step is only the beginning, for fear has a tendency to return to haunt us. I'll come back to this point later in greater detail in step 6, found in the latter part of this book. For now, let us examine how, in order to thrive in an ever-changing economy and world, we must reimagine the game and our role in it.

Today, our economy is a mixed bag: low unemployment and increasing numbers of opportunities but a gaping disparity between the very rich and the very poor, a gap wider than it has ever been before. As the recession of the early 1980s subsided, I entered the training and placement field, first as a career counselor and job developer and later, after receiving my master's degree, within a private practice where I integrated expressive arts therapy and career-life planning. The unemployment rate had declined, and industries that had long been hungry for workers, especially in new and emerging industries, grew starved to fill positions in which considerable growth had taken place. Meanwhile, many job seekers stood at the periphery, facing in the wrong direction, feeling ill equipped to traverse the gulf between themselves and a much-desired sense of security imagined as stable, long-term employment. Surely, they imagined, some company would take care of them; if only they knew where to go to get the new skills they required. Many still hold on to such hopes today.

Unfortunately, the answer to the plea implied in this scene is not straightforward. In most cases, when the iron mill closed, another iron mill did not open up on the other side of town. Neither did a different kind of mill open, requiring a simple upgrade of skills to operate new machines. Perhaps nothing opened up at all. The fact is, not only have the rules of the game changed, the entire game has changed. What worked twenty, ten, or even five years ago does not work anymore.

It may be misplaced to characterize changes in the economy as good or bad. What may be more important is to understand the new shape of an economy that has undergone enormous transformation and to explore ways to maneuver within it and even to influence its further development. People with talents exist, and in the wisdom of the universe, needs for individual talents also exist. The bringing together of the two is a primary focus of this book.

Many jobs have yet to be created and defined. This day and age calls us to take greater responsibility to define our own career paths. It may seem a foreboding task, but it can also be an exciting opportunity. On a global scale, the power of individuals to imagine possibilities can have an enormous impact. One day not so long ago, Richard and Maurice McDonald partnered with Ray Kroc to launch an idea about a previously unheard-of thing called fast food, and now the world's landscape is covered with golden arches. (See the film *The Founder*, 2017.)

Imagine Employers

Once upon a time, a dominant myth of the workplace held that middle-class Americans could depend upon their employers to take care of them. It was not at all unusual for an individual to offer up his or her labor to a company, which in turn would provide long-term security, defined as a job to go to every day, a living wage, and a pension to follow into retirement.

Rapid change in our current economy, including the tenuousness with which companies thrive from day to day, has necessitated a change in this myth. This was already true when I published the first edition of this book. Since that time, the economy has continued to evolve and change—sadly, not in favor of working America. As noted, the gap between the very wealthy and the rest of us continues to grow. Minimum wage has not kept up with inflation, and many working people now have trouble providing for the most basic needs for food, health care, and housing. Moreover, while unemployment rates have decreased generally, they have risen for marginalized groups, particularly black and Hispanic workers. A lengthy explanation of the reasons and possible solutions for this state of affairs extends beyond the scope of this book. I recommend reading Bernie Sanders's *The Decline of the Middle Class* and *Ending a Rigged Economy,* part 2, chapters 2 and 3 in *Bernie Sanders: Our Revolution* (2016, 206–317). Such background will help you better appreciate the broader social context and your place in it. It may lead to the avocation of political activism, certainly one legitimate way to assist in opening up opportunities for yourself and others.

Over time, our values in the United States have changed as well. When mass production reined in manufacturing, employers placed a high value on loyalty and conformity among workers. We are in a new age. Growth industries today recognize the trend toward more individualized, customized, and personalized service and the profitability of placing a higher value on qualities like originality, imagination, and an entrepreneurial spirit. With increasing threats facing our planet, people have become more environmentally conscious as well, and this heightened awareness of pollution in our water, food, air, and atmosphere has also shaped new industries and new ways of operating in existing ones. Rapid change in the world requires more flexibility, creativity, and leadership among workers able to see better ways of doing things.

Seeing change as frightening and unwanted may be a natural response, and it may be tempting to cast blame upon the Employer (with a capital *E*) for the insecurity some of us feel in the world of work, for it is the Employer who has assumed the more powerful role in the past. In an archetypal sense, this phenomenon of being forced out of a corporate nest can be experienced as facing abandonment from an authoritarian father. While there does appear to be a trend toward reestablishing authoritarianism in the world, I do not believe that old myth will work in our new age—at least not for long. Clearly a segment of the population wishes to hang on to the old myth; the election of an extremely authoritarian president may be seen as an example of that. The consequences of this choice will become more apparent in time, and in righting the ship that is our country, we may all need to step up in ways we've never had to before. Not an easy task, to be sure—but a necessary and inevitable one if we are to evolve in our consciousness and become better stewards of the world in which we live.

Shifting from a myth that values reliance on an external caretaker to one that necessitates self-reliance requires that we change the way we imagine employers and the way we imagine ourselves and our roles. Expectations determine the way we choose careers and move within the job market. Many of us sense this instinctively. We know that we can no longer depend upon any employer for a sense of security in the same way we previously did. We may also jump to the conclusion that any hope of enjoying security no longer exists. Not so! With the changing mythology, we must simply seek and find security elsewhere, namely within ourselves and within our communities.

In the first edition of this book, I created a cartoon to illustrate to some job developers I was training the way many of us imagine employers. Notice how the cartoon image on the right portrays the Employer as a powerful and domineering force. What would happen if we reversed the image; how would that look and feel in contrast to this one?

An employer/employee relationship actually works best when the two are posed eye to eye, when a more egalitarian relationship or partnership is conveyed, at least in terms of our mutual humanity, worth, and the extent to which both are deserving of respect.

Oh, Great Employer, I am not worthy!

Figure 1. How we might imagine an Employer

Imagine the pendulum swinging even a little bit in the other direction and the impact of that different worldview. Suddenly, the expectation that the employer would be doing you a favor to hire you is turned on its head. Instead, you may begin to appreciate how fortunate that employer and company would be to have you on board.

This is not a simple mind game. Employers hire people because of their distinct abilities to contribute. Employees are creative problem solvers, need-meeters and profit-makers. The most successful in this day and age tend to be proactive and entrepreneurial in their approach.

> *Employers hire people because of their distinct abilities to contribute. Employees are creative problem solvers, need-meeters and profit-makers.*

Imagine Yourself

When we imagine employers as our caretakers, we tend to attach our identities—or at least our career identities—to them. We introduce ourselves in those terms; for example, "Hi, I'm Tammy—I'm an electrician at Acme." When we shift to a mode of self-reliance, our identity becomes more personal. We might identify equally with other roles we play in life, "Hi, I'm Jose; I'm an avid baseball fan and the proud father of this little one, here—oh, and I teach at the high school, too."

On the next page, you will find a simple exercise to try.

I purposely chose a corporation here with a reputation for being a powerful company that takes good care of its people. Of course, that phrase is open to interpretation. One could argue that employers who truly care for their employees seek not to create an insular and inescapable environment but rather to support the personal and professional growth and development of people and to take genuine pleasure in seeing them advance, even when it takes them outside the company. Employers subscribing to Bob Greenleaf's servant-leadership model come to mind; some outstanding examples include Southwest Airlines, Starbucks, T. D. Industries, and others.

Exercise 2: The "SICK-y"

Imagine you are currently working as a salesperson for a large corporation called Springfield Important Computer Klatch (SICK). SICK has a reputation for taking extremely good care of its people. It typically takes people with limited education and skills, trains them in their own particular methods (and jargon), and promotes them to high-paying salaried positions. Suppose now that you find yourself at a social event. As you are introduced to other partygoers, think about how you might respond to the question, "What do you do?" Look at this continuum of statements:

- "I'm a SICK-y."
- "I work for Springfield Important Computers."
- "I have a knack for selling user-friendly software to computer-unfriendly people."
- "I'm a devoted husband, a computer buff, and I make the best chili in Springfield."

Which type of statement have you used most in your experience?

Which way of communicating who you are suits you best?

Which would you like to use more?

Needless to say, caring employers who fairly compensate their employees and who generously acknowledge and reward excellence are somewhat rare and therefore particularly hard to separate from. People who work for such companies may take great pride in naming their employer as a primary part of their identity. People thrive within these cultures, at least for a time. But many a devoted employee has experienced layoffs when profits dip, or products become obsolete, or income sources are not diversified, or the company just cannot keep up with rapid change in the economic landscape. Such casualties may have a tougher time than others grieving their losses and readjusting to a new place in the workforce. Some unique work cultures can become so ingrained that other potential employers may indeed have trouble understanding the jargon the workers speak or translating skill sets in a meaningful way. To reference our imaginary scenario in exercise 2, résumés may read like SICK résumés—great for a SICK employee but more troublesome for other settings.

The emotional impact of being laid off in such situations can be devastating. Being abandoned by a powerful, authoritarian "father" and facing the never-suspected prospect of needing to find a new place to land can be terrifying, and it can require a period of healing and rejuvenation.

Returning to that imaginary scenario, suppose you are the corporate salesperson named, and you have just been laid off. Now what do you say at that party? It may take some time before you are able to shed the SICK identity—to move on from "I used to be a SICK-y" to "I'm a dad, a computer buff, and a great chili maker." Traversing this path is a process of realizing "I am not my job; I am more than a job." Consider how much easier it would be to move into another job from the latter attitude.

For most, many avenues may exist that could potentially meet our needs to feel fulfilled and allow us to use our unique talents. In the final analysis, the success you experience today depends less on who helps you than upon who you are and on how this measures up to how you have defined success for yourself.

Imagine Success

Let us turn briefly to a discussion of what it means to be successful.

Each of us has a different view of success, and our ideas are influenced to varying degrees by many things—ego-based needs and wants; the desires that others (such as parents and other significant relationships) have for us, some of which we have so fully integrated that we experience them as our own internal motivations; pressures imposed by what we see in the media; and in some cases a vague or crystal-clear awareness of being called by a divine or collective need or higher intelligence. Experiences of bliss will give us cues in that latter direction.

Let us begin with a nod to ego and think about how we define success off the tops of our heads. The following exercise can guide the process.

Exercise 3: How You Imagine Success

Take a sheet of paper oriented horizontally, or fill in the template below. Along the left-hand margin, make a list of five to seven things you feel are essential to success (in no particular order). Across the top of the page, write the numbers 1 through 6, with 1 signifying *low* and 6 *high*. Now rate yourself on each of the items by aligning a dot with each appropriate rating, honestly reflecting upon where you are today. Finally, connect the dots. (See the example on the next page.)

	(Low)				(High)
	1	2	3	4	5	6
1. _____
2. _____
3. _____
4. _____
5. _____
6. _____
7. _____

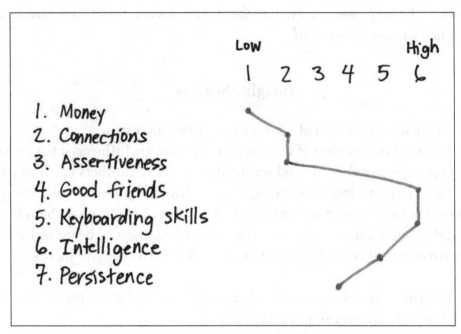

Figure 2. Nora's success list and self-assessment

Note how the individual described above (we'll call her Nora) has defined success. Based on her definition, she is partially successful, since she has evaluated herself as being bright, with many good friends and excellent keyboarding skills. She further assesses herself as not being terribly persistent, even less assertive, having few connections and limited financial resources. Put yourself in Nora's shoes. What would you do?

To most people, the answer seems obvious. Traditional wisdom would probably have Nora grabbing the first job she sees, in order to get immediate income, taking a class in assertiveness training, and cold calling around to make some of those networking connections she now feels are so important.

Suppose Nora tries all these things. What do you expect will follow? In my experience, it often follows a course something like this: Nora takes the first job she finds, at a convenience store down the street. She works alone most of the time and feels rather insecure about her work, as it is new to her. But she keeps telling herself, "It's only temporary."

Nora signs up for an evening assertiveness training class in which the instructor encourages her to "think positively" and to speak up for herself. The instructor teaches her to stand up straight and to use her voice in a manner that evokes more confidence. The class is extremely difficult for Nora; she is in awe of the instructor but feels like a fish out of water. She has never been very persistent (as noted), and she considers quitting, but she is afraid this is her only hope. As for cold calling, despite good intentions, Nora never seems to get around to it, and guilt plagues her for this "failure."

Meanwhile, Nora entirely neglects her strengths—her keyboarding skills and small but devoted circle of friends.

A few weeks later, she rates herself on the same scale and finds that except for a small increase in her income, things have gotten worse. What happened?

Let us suppose Nora had taken the opposite approach. Suppose she invested the lion's share of her attention and energies into those things for which she gave herself high ratings. Let us suppose, for example, that she dusted off her laptop, got hold of some genealogy and self-publishing software she had never used but always wanted to learn, and started keyboarding two or three hours every day, writing up her family's history. Let us also suppose she made a point of calling at least one friend every day and planning two (frugal) outings or visits a week.

Chances are, the entire scale would rise. Nora would find that in addition to increasing her keyboarding speed and accuracy, and in addition to learning a new software program and engaging in a project that would offer new avenues for connecting with her own family history and with loved ones, she would also discover an increased assertiveness in herself. This emerged as a natural by-product of engaging in activities she already enjoyed and in which she already felt some confidence. Moreover, she would find that by engaging her closest friends in discussions about personal projects close to her heart and her hopes and dreams, she would have sparked their imaginations, gotten them excited about and involved in her job search, and she would have further expanded her personal network, or *connections*, to use her term. Quite likely, a more fitting job would also follow in time.

The purpose of thinking through this exercise is to shine light upon how following bliss can fuel existing strengths while working with or accommodating to natural limitations—without judgment.

The key is to first understand and embrace all of a person's qualities. In my view, we all have dominant qualities and traits; some aspects serve us well, while others present potential risks or liabilities. This holistic approach differs fundamentally from a deficit-based approach (focused on fixing what is "wrong") or even an abundance-based approach (focused on either ignoring what is wrong or turning those negatives into positives).

Following bliss requires some relearning, or at least some reframing, since popular culture seems intent on guiding people toward those deficit-based or, more recently, abundance-based approaches.

Let us begin with the radical assumption that nothing is wrong. Rather, things are as they are, and our challenge is to make the most of what we have—to work *with* all we have, not work *around* it, and indeed, like an artist, to "make something out of it."

Reframing Strengths and Weaknesses

Just out of undergraduate school, I took a job I loved. The only drawback to the position was finding myself in a somewhat tense relationship with the director of the agency in which the program was housed. We were able to work together pretty well despite different working styles and different personalities. Then, as a courtesy, my outside supervisor invited the agency director's input in my annual performance review.

I had done outstanding work since being hired, and the performance review reflected that. Then, at the end of the review form, under "areas in need of improvement," I found myself taken aback when I read the comment that described me as being "aloof" around other staff.

I was young and ambitious and eager to do well, and the comment took the wind out of my sails. It seemed to me that this person had gone out of her way to find something to complain about. But I set aside my astonishment, anger, and pride and chose to examine what grain of truth might lie in those words.

After some reflection, I was able to understand how the director may have arrived at her remark. I knew that I was able to bring an exceptionally attentive presence to the clients with whom I worked; however, I was not the type of person inclined to socialize at the water fountain. Most of the time, I dove into my work with a deliberateness and concentration that left little time for lunch and bathroom breaks, never mind small talk. It was easy for me to imagine myself busily writing at a computer terminal and not even noticing a passerby offering a morning greeting. Could this be interpreted as aloofness? Probably. How far was I willing to go to change myself? Not very far. I was unwilling to give up a part of myself that had served me well in my life. I could certainly make an effort to make my personal style known to people, so they would not feel I was purposely snubbing them. I could even make an effort to take a break once in a while to check on how other people were doing. But I refused on principle to become someone I was not. Giving up this quality would have meant giving up a gift I had for completing huge volumes of work with great efficiency, and I still had a lot of work I wanted to do.

What I learned from this experience was that we all have dominant qualities that help to define us as individuals, though these qualities can be malleable to a certain extent. These dominant qualities can be our greatest strengths as well as our greatest weaknesses. They are qualities that have many aspects and manifest differently in different situations. It will behoove you to take stock of your own so you can better assess and appreciate what you have to offer the world—and better communicate it. Ultimately, this awareness helps you find your most fitting niche. You are certainly better off in terms of your personal happiness and also in terms of the betterment of the world when you fully embrace the unique individual you are.

One way to start this self-exploration is to embark on an exploration of personality. I have been particularly impressed with the Nine Point System, or NPS (also known by the term *Enneagram*) as a vehicle for self-understanding and for appreciating and learning to work with differences among people. I highly recommend Dr. Tina Thomas's book, *Who Do You Think You Are?* (2016). But if you are impatient, you might hop on the Internet to take a short test that will help you determine your own personality type. Log on to www.9types.com, and look under the "tests" bar for the "New Test by Tal." This will open up a self-inventory that will only take a few minutes. Ideally, you may then print off or copy your numbers and take them to someone with expertise in the NPS to help you interpret the numbers. But a quick read through the personality descriptions will give you some basic understanding and tips.

On the following page, you will find an exercise to help you get started with understanding your own dominant qualities through the "weakness" aspect. Sadly, many people seem far more aware of (and in some cases obsessed with) their perceived weaknesses than their strengths. This unfortunate state of affairs makes this approach a relatively easy or quick point of access to understanding dominant qualities, particularly for people on the lower end of the self-esteem scale.

Exercise 4: Exploring Dominant Qualities

Think about a personal trait you have defined as a weakness. Externalize the thing and give it substance. That is, draw it, shape it in a lump of clay, write a poem or song that captures its essence, or render a scene in a sand tray that describes it. Take some time to reflect upon what you have created. Then, describe the thing to someone else or write down your description without trying to relate it to your current experience. (In other words, "stay with the image"; define it in its own terms.) Engage in a dialogue with the image, and ask the following questions. Be receptive to whatever answers may come.

What or who are you?

Where did you come from, and how is it that you have you appeared to me?

How do you serve me?

What challenges, opportunities, and dangers do you present?

What do you have to teach me?

What do you have that I need?

Let us walk through an example of someone who engaged this exercise. Sean feels uncomfortable in large groups of people he does not know well. He shares an apartment with a gregarious gentleman, Tito, who frequently boasts of all the great contacts he makes at parties and networking events. Tito serves as a relentless reminder to Sean of his own tendency to shy away from large groups, and Sean perceives that as a weakness.

After identifying this "weakness," Sean begins to meticulously paint an image of a room filled with upwardly mobile men and women bearing cell phones and buzzing with conversation. He places himself in a corner with his back to the wall and a look of terror on his face. Already this rich material lends opportunities to learn a great deal about Sean—his careful manner, his ability to manipulate art materials skillfully, the fact that he does not particularly care for the type of cell-phone-toting people portrayed in his image, who on further reflection seem shallow and self-serving to him.

When asked to be more specific about his "shyness" and what it looks like, Sean elaborates, and an honest dialogue ensues:

Sean: Shyness hovers in the room. It is a cloud, a barrier between me and others.

Therapist: How does the barrier serve you?

Sean: It protects me from being taken in by people I cannot trust.

Therapist: Does the barrier follow you everywhere?

Sean: No, only places where I feel vulnerable.

Therapist:	Describe the cloud in more detail.
Sean:	Soft—like cotton, but I can put my hand through it. I could even walk through it if I wished.
Therapist:	It sounds pleasant, and as though you have some control over it.
Sean:	Yes. It's actually quite warm and comforting.
Therapist:	If it could speak to you, what do you think the cloud would say?
Sean:	Hello there, Sean!
Therapist:	So the barrier is more friend than foe? What if it did not exist?
Sean:	Hmm—I think I really need it there.

This is an abbreviated version of a dialogue that could lend more and more insights when further pursued. But already it is clear that Sean's shyness serves him by offering a protective boundary that he can, in fact, transcend when he wishes to connect with others.

We all need boundaries, and not all of us manage them as well as Sean. Can you think of any occupations where this quality might be an asset? How about a person who must deal with sensitive and confidential material?

Take heed from this example. It is very important to make the most of who we are, for the universe requires us all. Imagine how dull and uninspired life would be if we were able to change our basic attributes with the push of a button, eliminating the ones we find too challenging. Imagine the lessons we would never learn, the joys we would never know.

What Personality Is Not

Be careful here not to confuse personality traits with feelings. Personality consists of enduring traits that help to define individuals. They might include introversion, charisma, acute sensitivity, or a tendency to value intellectual ways of knowing over intuition. On the other hand, things like sadness, fear, and lack of motivation are not personality traits at all but rather feelings, very much dependent on circumstances and prone to coming and going.

Time and again, people we know counsel us about what employers want: enthusiasm, commitment, initiative, motivation, stick-to-itiveness, to name a few. Too often, we think of these qualities as personality traits. In other words, we either have them or we don't. But all these traits lie within every human being's repertoire. We may manifest them in different ways, but regardless of our style in expressing enthusiasm, for example, people will recognize it when they witness it. Notwithstanding the "7" personality, known as the Enthusiast, is particularly known for naturally expressing this trait in a rather enduring way, the ability to feel enthusiastic about things with which we resonate comes naturally to all humans. Wayne Dyer (2014) reminds us that enthusiasm derives from a word origin that can be translated as "the God within." Enthusiasm can be understood as the burning in a burning desire; not a function of personality but a function of how we feel.

This is good news, indeed! For it means that these highly valued attitudes, though we might express them differently, are within everyone's reach. Think about a time in your life when you felt enthusiastic about something. If you have never felt enthusiasm, I feel bad for you, but hear this: That is not because of who you are. It is because of how you feel. Perhaps you or others around you have put dampers on whatever it is that might spark your enthusiasm. I am giving you permission now to tear them down. I insist upon it. Remember, it is not only your right to know bliss and to pursue it, but it is also your responsibility. You are robbing the rest of the world as well as yourself if you ignore it.

Recalling times in our lives when we felt tuned in to our truest senses of ourselves is a critical step in the career search, and many of the career-life planning exercises in this book are based on this premise. I will share a few of these in step 3. But first, let us make a brief visit to whatever misery we may be holding on to.

COMING TO TERMS WITH THE MISERY

If I stay in this job, I'm afraid I'll end up hurting someone.
I'm so filled with rage—and these days, it doesn't take much to set me off.

Harry was a story on the evening news waiting to happen when he came to the first meeting of my More-than-a-Job Club seminar. I was accustomed to beginning these seminars by giving people the opportunity to vent whatever grievances they might have carried in with them. I was not sure that the holding environment I had created in the seminar structure was adequate for containing the rage Harry brought with him, and I considered making a referral to some outside counseling. But in this case, the group turned out to be a manageable size and quickly established a trusting environment, impressively eager to accompany this troubled soul on his quest.

Harry's story told of being denied a promotion that had been given to a younger gentleman, allegedly with an inside connection to the company, a man Harry felt was less competent than he. Harry had come to the seminar with the intent of getting out of the job as soon as he could, before he acted in a manner he would later regret.

In the first session, each group member shared experiences of anger and frustration, not only with words, but in creative writing and artwork. By externalizing grievances in words and images, we can relate to the content in new ways and deepen our understanding of the images as well as the myths and dynamics they describe (Knill, Barba, and Fuchs 1995).

I watched as Harry stood back and regarded the material he had put out, and we all listened with interest as he talked about his writing and sketches. We did not analyze the words and images; we simply witnessed their unfoldment. The images were no longer stuck like a broken record; they had shifted like the dynamic entities they were, richer with each new rendering and observation.

The following week, we began the process of in-depth self-inventorying. When his turn came, Harry reported a startling change in his workplace that had begun in the previous week. He no longer dreaded showing up at his workplace; he said he no longer feared losing control, was able to leave his work "at the office," and actually found small ways to enjoy some of his workday. His only explanation for the change was the cathartic experience he had of putting his anger out on the table in the previous session, along with receiving others' support and perspectives.

When you feel unrest or dissonance, it may be a cue to pause and reflect—rather than to avoid the material, and in turn to end up repressing or projecting it. There is no way to rush this process, and sometimes it takes longer than others. But there is no substitute for an honest appraisal and integration before moving on. Every time we try to avoid the things that haunt us, they tend to return with even greater insistence (Fox 1988).

> *Every time we try to avoid the things that haunt us, they tend to return with even greater insistence.*

Garrett McAuliffe (1993, 36) calls this first, cathartic stage of career exploration "acknowledging dissonant voices." I have found this critical stage serves several important purposes. For example, it

- permits a cleansing catharsis of feelings of anger, disappointment, guilt, frustration, grief, confusion, and/or whatever else might be demanding attention;
- allows for the initial development of rapport between people and opportunities to listen and support each other;
- opens the door to change—that is, when you confront how awful things may be, it becomes more difficult to ignore them and do nothing;
- allows for the development of a more complete perspective on one's situation or the ability to see the "big picture" (e.g., "I am not my anger. I am more than my anger.");
- offers some initial insights into what has not worked in the past and, therefore, what might work better in the future; and
- facilitates letting go and moving on from a place of stasis.

This is the time to indulge in all the pains and agonies that have stood in the way of moving forward. It is not a time to rush forward into "getting over it" or "making nice." The unpleasant material deserves a fair hearing and full acknowledgment before an individual moves on to problem-solve and set new goals. There is much to be learned in the telling of and dialoguing with "tales of woe."

Again, I encourage art-making at this stage in the process. I have found that presenting material in a collage or sculpture, for example, can be liberating and for some, much easier than trying to find words to convey painful stories and the feelings associated with them. When images emerge, they always bring new, sometimes surprising information and, especially in dialogue, a richer and fuller understanding of familiar touchstones that return at various stages of the career search to inform our perspectives on stumbling blocks and successes.

Once a person has had an opportunity to acknowledge the pain of losses incurred, it is important to honor and make room for a grieving process. Everyone has a different way of coping with grief. Art materials can assist in the process in a variety of ways. One important task involves a careful review and reflection upon the legacies of the former job, including the gifts one takes from the experience (lessons learned, skills acquired, relationships forged, achievements, and so on). It also involves things one may need to let go of (an obsolete skill set no longer needed in the world, spaces and places to which one will not be returning, and so forth). Grounding such a review in an art-making activity offers a vehicle or ritual for acceptance and moving on from grief, and it can be engaged through reflective conversation, writing in a journal, creating a song or poem that summarizes the experience, even drawing or painting a timeline. An exercise of which I am particularly fond is the "altered book." An art therapist could help you with this; I'll include basic instructions.

Exercise 5: Making an Altered Book for Acceptance and Moving On

Find an old book that you might have otherwise discarded (perhaps that employee handbook you don't need anymore). Don't worry about damage; this process will repurpose and rejuvenate the book. Page through to see if there are any particular phrases or pictures you want to be sure to keep, and mark them. Then, using a strong adhesive, glue together some of the pages, especially if they are thin and flimsy, taking care to avoid those marked elements. Now, gesso all the unmarked pages (that is, cover them all in white gesso paint), and gesso around any elements you want to keep.

When the gesso has dried, paint (acrylic works well) and/or paste collage images (photos, newspaper and magazine clippings, original drawings, candy wrappers, colorful ribbons, etc.) onto the pages in a way that tells your story. A variety of mixed media can be used to make your altered book, particularly on the cover, where you might experiment with colored tape, fabric, wallpaper, beads, perhaps a material used by the company you have left. Be creative!

When finished, share your finished product and talk through it with a trusted therapist, friend, family member, or members of an expressive arts group.

Image credit for altered book to Rachelle Barmann

STEP 3

GETTING IN TOUCH WITH BLISS

You will never be able to escape from your heart,
so it is better to listen to what it has to say.
—Paul Coelho, *The Alchemist*

In 1995, I attended a presentation by futurist Ed Barlow. He spoke convincingly and at length, with no small measure of passion, about the enormous uncertainty the future held. He spoke about rapid advances in technology and observed that fully half the jobs to be had in this country in the year 2000 did not even exist then. A quick look back over the past two decades demonstrates how right he was. New changes continue to unfold at every turn today.

Mr. Barlow urged those present not to rest in complacency but rather to position ourselves and actively prepare for a future already upon us. A frustrated executive in attendance then stood and asked, "But how can I plan in an environment of uncertainty?" The plea gave us all pause, including Mr. Barlow, who deferred the question to the latter part of his presentation. He did return to the point, albeit briefly, and he suggested an approach of "scanning and evaluating" all that we saw happening around us.

This was certainly an important part of the answer. However, it did not seem to satisfy the crowd fully. I imagined that the executive who had asked the question might have answered, "What is the point of scanning and evaluating the present? I need to anticipate five or more years down the road!" I sensed a general consensus that the problem was a difficult one for which there simply existed no better solution than the one Barlow had offered.

But there is more to this than meets the eye. Scan and evaluate the present, yes. Yet more than this, we need to fine-tune our sensitivity and learn to trust our intuitions about the future. These intuitions may be as subtle as a feeling of being passionately drawn to a thing without understanding why. It is the *Follow Your Bliss!* approach put into action on a day-to-day basis. Every yearning, however great or small, emerges in synchronicity with a corresponding need in the universe. A spiritual self-awareness therefore includes an awareness of and faithfulness to these yearnings. Wisdom exists in gut feelings and in bliss, and if we trust and follow their calls—which we can recognize in feelings of passion, excitement, and burning desire—then that wisdom will be revealed in time. In following bliss, we not only reap the rewards of personal satisfaction, but we also identify and meet real needs in the world around us. I learned this lesson in my own life.

My career path began at an early age. I had a passion for many things as a young person, and I felt despair when others more experienced than I advised me to "choose one." I remember an assignment in the first grade: "Draw what you want to be when you grow up." Even then, I could not choose. I stubbornly put a line through the middle of the paper. Then I drew a singer on one side and a teacher on the other.

I was fascinated by human beings and passionate about the arts. I loved the arts, not only music, and I sensed their connectedness and showed talents in many branches—music, sculpture, drawing, dance, and creative writing, to name a few.

I began my college career in a traditional music therapy program, which was a partial integration of my interests. But I found it too restrictive. In my second year, I transferred to a more flexible, design-your-own-major program (the "Paracollege" of St. Olaf College in Northfield, Minnesota), and I crafted an integrated curriculum that led me to combine a study of the arts and psychology. Upon concluding that undergraduate degree, I listened to my gut and took a paraprofessional position in an employment and training program for people with epilepsy (TAPS, the Training and Placement Service). I stayed there almost six years, honing both my career counseling and administrative skills, for in time I was asked to direct the national program.

With no place further to go in that job, after a few years I hungered for an advanced degree. By this time, I had learned of a graduate program in psychotherapy that promoted an integrated arts approach, the Expressive Therapies program at Lesley College Graduate School in Cambridge, Massachusetts.

Mind you, I loved the job I was leaving. I was better paid than most of my same-age peers, and the work itself fed a real passion. I looked forward to going to work each day. Those looking from the outside in tried to appeal to my "rationality" by advising, "So why don't you keep your job and study at night; and if you love your work so much, why don't you get an advanced degree in vocational rehabilitation?"

They meant well, but I could not follow their advice. Those options held no spark for me; I hungered for something different. I could not explain the logic in it, for the reasons burst from my heart, not from my intellect. I was called. In a decision that I thought at the time might very well sever any further connection with the world I had grown to love so much, I quit my job, rented a U-Haul, and moved myself to Massachusetts to rekindle the artist's spirit in me.

The arts and psychotherapy training was difficult, emotionally demanding, and exceedingly rewarding. The relationships I forged were precious and lasting. When I finished, I emerged (to my surprise) not as a "new" person shaped into a new form by the training I had received, but rather as the same person with all the same passions, but with a broader repertoire of skills. As if by magic, the training had become fully integrated into the person I was. I felt the spiritual awareness that I was becoming even more the person I was intended to be. I was no Frasier (the television psychologist), nor was I the psychiatrist portrayed by Judd Hirsch in *Ordinary People*, nor was I Sybil's therapist, as portrayed by Joanne Woodward. These were images I carried with me early in my training of people working as psychotherapists. Young people today may carry more updated images—of therapists portrayed in movies like *Antwon Fischer* or *Silver Linings Playbook*, or even an image like the burned-out social worker in the film *The Joker*.

As for me, I was my own person. And I continually encourage my students to find out who they are as well. When it came to career-life planning in particular, I had some fresh ideas to share. How pleasantly surprised I was to find that my particular blend of talents and training had uniquely equipped me to fill a hungry niche in the field. The marriage of talents seems so sensible and clear to me now, but this awareness came only after I took the risk to enter and complete that clinical training and to establish a private practice. I had something fresh and new to offer this field I loved.

The career of my husband at the time held similar surprises. After years of working successfully in news radio (which he loved), he felt it was time for a change. He took a risk and quit his job to work in his father's plumbing business. He obtained his journeyman's license, while he anguished (just a little) over how to spend the rest of his work life. What, after all, did communications and plumbing have in common—particularly if you factored in his gregarious personality and a natural penchant for entertaining?

He found his perfect niche, too—that of a national training manager for a large manufacturer of plumbing and heating equipment. He was always an animated trainer, and he loved being in the spotlight. The expertise he acquired in the plumbing and heating product line, along with some basic skills in installation, made him the perfect candidate for that line of work. It also offered far greater room for advancement and more financial remuneration than anything he had done to date. Perhaps more importantly, he was fully in his element in this line of work. He still loves and benefits from the risks he took back then.

Following bliss can impact not only individuals but also entire industries. Not long ago, I read wisdom in the calls of a number of younger peers in the field of expressive arts therapy. While teaching second-year graduate students at Lesley University, I became aware of the phenomenon as the brainstorm of a student in my thesis seminar. She had left a successful career as a restaurateur to study expressive arts therapy. She had a dream of one day creating a dining/therapeutic environment that would be surrounded by art and make available to patrons seductive art materials and opportunities to be creative. At about the same time, I learned of another student who was trying (without much success, as it happened) to get approval to write a thesis on an "expressive arts therapy café" model. Her thesis instructor was concerned at the time that the material was "not clinical enough"; that is, it did not fit the established paradigm for how people could or should use their talents as expressive arts therapists. A third student, also at precisely the same time, actually started up an "expressive arts therapy café" on campus. It became a meeting place for students to create and share art and also to nourish themselves with good food and drink in an informal environment.

None of these students knew each other. Each of them probably felt she had an original idea—and each had a decided passion for that idea. This was bliss! The idea was bigger than the sum of individuals. The impulse came as a response to a need in the universe for a nourishing haven and creative outlet for people stressed out with their high-tech, low-touch lives.

If anything, the level of stress among the general public has only increased over the past several years. In the world at large, I see similar models continuing to pop up in various places. "Paint and sip" wine and art-making classes seem to be particularly popular, but art-inspired restaurants of various types can be found all around the country.

This scenario is by no means isolated either. Ed Barlow (1995) pointed out even in the mid-1990s that most of the growth happening in the labor market happened across industries. Successful companies were even then stepping outside established routines in big and small ways and integrating diverse thinking and activities.

The *Follow Your Bliss!* approach is important not only for big decisions. It is important to weigh our passion, even as we plan a daily schedule. When we assess what is important to us as we set about writing a five-year plan, for example, we need to be sure that we translate our aspirations into daily tasks. We must make sure that we can find enjoyment every day and never do anything merely as a means to an end. I have known too many people who have suffered through a formal education with the fantasy that what came out on the other end would be worth the agony—and instead continued to be miserable. Let your own bliss be the beacon that guides you ultimately and day by day.

The ability to get in touch with feelings of bliss forms a foundation for most of what remains in this book. There are different ways of doing this. One way is to simply live mindfully, to notice and pay attention to joy when it emerges naturally in the course of a day, and to use the awareness of joy as a beacon to guide you forward.

Bliss is your guiding light, your north star. It will direct you to work that is meaningful and needed in the world, work that will bring you fulfillment and joy. For many, it can be elusive, however. Creating spaces conducive to the emergence of bliss, creating spaces where we can reconnect with bliss, may be the best place to start.

Priming Yourself

I strongly recommend daily meditation to develop a state of mind open to bliss, willing to embrace it, and able to recognize it in daily life. Many meditation videos are available on the web. Deepak Chopra offers an excellent one that works nicely. (See https://m.youtube.com/watch?v=XSNpGyG2jSw.) In this fifteen-minute guided meditation, Chopra suggests the Sanskrit mantra, "Sat Chit Ananda," which roughly translates to "Living Your Bliss" or your rapture.

Exercise 6: A Guided Meditation for Connecting with Bliss

Find a quiet place where you won't be interrupted. You may choose to sit or lie down; it's up to you. As you get comfortable, close your eyes, and take three deep, long breaths, inhaling to the count of four, and exhaling to the count of four. Feel more relaxed with every breath you take.

Inhale – two – three – four.
Exhale – two – three – four.
Inhale – two – three – four.
Exhale – two – three – four.
Inhale – two – three – four.
Exhale – two – three – four.

Now begin to observe the inflow and outflow of your breath. With each inhalation and exhalation, allow yourself to become more relaxed, more comfortable, more at peace.

As stray thoughts come to you, acknowledge their presence, and let them go, returning your attention to observing the natural flow of your breathing.

Feeling even more relaxed now, bring to mind a time when you felt most completely yourself, ...being who you were always meant to be, ...engaging in activities perfectly suited to who you are. Experience this blissful state in all the detail you can imagine—the smells, ...sounds, ...images, ...tactile sensations, ...and even the way your body feels moving in this state.

Stay with the feeling of bliss, while the music continues, until the bell signals the end of the meditation. Again, as stray thoughts come to you, acknowledge their presence, and let them go, returning your attention to observing the natural flow of your breathing.

[Ring a soft bell to signal the beginning of the remainder of the meditation. Allow 15 minutes to pass, then ring the bell one more time to signal the end of the meditation.]

You may record the above script to guide your meditation. Play some soft, meditative music in the background as you read the script to provide a container for the meditative experience.

As noted, once you develop a habit of living in a manner that is open to bliss, you will be able to identify it more readily as you work through the remaining exercises in this book and also as you move about in the world. If you prefer a guided meditation more aligned with your spiritual beliefs, I am sure you can find it, often at no cost at all; there is something for everyone on the Internet.

The Burns Sensual Awareness Inventory (SAI)

Another approach to encountering experiences of bliss is to examine the ways in which we engage with the world through our various senses. George Burns (1998) developed a simple inventory for connecting with joy through nature. Despite the simplicity of this exercise, it can elicit powerful responses. Based on the premise that we encounter joy primarily through our senses, these simple questions encourage a connection or reconnection with them.

I was first introduced to this exercise by Bea Keller-Dupree at an Association for Creativity in Counseling (ACC) conference (2016). Dr. Keller-Dupree adapted the Burns assessment by adding an additional space for "activities," which seemed to round out the tool well. I include my very similar version on the following page.

Exercise 7: Burns Sensual Awareness Inventory (SAI)

In the following chart, try to come up with ten items in each area that bring you joy and comfort. Share your results with a group or another person.

The Sensual Awareness Inventory (SAI)*

Vision ◉◉	Touch ✍
Taste ☺	**Sound** 👂
Smell 👃	**Kinesthetic Activity** 🏃

---

* Adapted by Dr. Haley Fox from Burns, George W. (George William) (1998). The sensual awareness inventory, in *Nature-guided therapy: Brief integrative strategies for health and well-being*. Brunner/Mazel, Philadelphia, PA, pp. 57-70.

The Sensual Awareness Inventory (SAI)[*]

Instructions for using the SAI:

Under each heading, take a few minutes to list or sketch items or activities that give you comfort, pleasure, and/or enjoyment. Burns recommends 10-20 items for each category, but try to focus on the quality of the experience over quantity. Use separate, larger sheets of paper or collage materials if desired.

Explore with a partner or group what you gained from the activity.

- What feelings, thoughts and early recollections emerged?
- What did the exercise teach you about your experience of comfort and pleasure?
- Did you learn anything new about yourself?
- Were there any surprises in what emerged?
- Are there things you might have expected to find on your list that did *not* show up?
- How much of your time do you actually spend currently in sensual engagement that brings you comfort and joy?

Consider how you can use the awareness you have gained.

- How can you build more comfort and enjoyment into your daily life?
- How can you apply this learning to your own professional self-care?
- What is something you can do *today* to increase your enjoyment?
- When might you use this tool again in the future?

---

[*] Adapted by Dr. Haley Fox from Burns, George W. (George William) (1998). The sensual awareness inventory, in *Nature-guided therapy: Brief integrative strategies for health and well-being.* Brunner/Mazel, Philadelphia, PA, pp. 57-70.

STEP 4

ART AND THE WAY TO
SELF-AWARENESS

Pay attention to the things you are naturally drawn to.
They are often connected to your path, passion, and purpose in life.
Have the courage to follow them.
—Ruben Chavez

In my view, there exists a fundamental flaw in the way career assessment has traditionally been conducted. Typically, to discover an appropriate career path, an individual is interviewed and/or given a written test, often consisting of multiple-choice questions and Likert rankings. A number of such assessments and inventories exist, and they do have their place. Martha Bowman prepared a nice collection (complete with links); this is available at http://www. marthabowman.info/my_complete_list.htm. Personal interviews are less formal and structured. But in both cases (written assessment or structured interview), inquiries are generally directed to the intellect.

When the intellect is engaged, responses we get can be misleading. Think about a personal experience you may have had with career assessment and guidance. Call to mind those popular checklists of "values," for example. Imagine how you might proceed through the list of values named and check off or prioritize those you find most important and least important to you; for example, "love" gets a number 1, "money" gets a 2, and "security" gets a 3. Then someone comes up with a new list with different options, and you start to reconsider your responses. You might be inclined to think, "Creativity—I hadn't thought of that one. That's important, too. I'll redo my list."

Another problem with this approach is the tendency for the intellect to zero in on things we have been told or taught. Someone may be taught that money is important and that being an accountant is the best path to money. If he or she never questions it, not only will that person name it as an important value, but he or she might also proceed with getting a degree and job in accounting. This would purely be a means to an imagined end, even while disliking the process every step of the way.

Questions that concern life and career are not matters of the intellect. They are matters of the heart. Therefore, the only insights into bliss, purpose, mission, talents, interests, and values I trust are those accessed not through the intellect but rather through the heart, the feeling center.

Nice idea, perhaps. But how is it done?

The approach I use is to begin any inquiry not with what someone thinks but with how that person feels. The best way to illustrate this is through some more exercises, like the writing and drawing exercises included in this chapter.

Incidentally, at this juncture, when one engages in self-exploration, the purpose is to gather in as much information as possible and not to rush to limit or nail down options. Later on, when endeavoring to give substance to images that emerge, the focus of step 5, it will become more important to focus and to narrow options.

This initial exploratory stage is a time for "stirring the soup." It is a time for being open and receptive to memories, images, and ideas and to trust that if they have arrived at your doorstep, they have purpose and meaning—even though you may not yet understand the purpose. Make room!

Individuals are many things, and there are many ways to frame who you are. I will focus here on three dimensions particularly pertinent to career-life planning: values, interests, and talents.

Values

We value what is important to us. Values may be culturally shaped to some extent, but they are also highly personal, and we generally hold on to our values with great intensity and emotion. Values define our limits. They form the lines we will not cross. Indeed, the image of a line drawn in the sand provides a useful imaginal anchor to help you get in touch with your values. By examining those line-crossing moments that arouse the most intense feelings and by closely examining what those responses might mean in the language of values, you increase your self-awareness, so important to getting matched to a successful job and career.

The exercise presented in the following pages is designed to walk you through the process of identifying values by identifying line-crossing moments as a starting point. A more detailed explanation follows the exercise found below.

Exercise 8: Clarifying Values

Values have to do with limits. They are the lines or boundaries we draw around ourselves beyond which we will not cross without risking feelings of guilt, psychic pain, or injury. This exercise is designed to help uncover those values of greatest personal importance.

1. Find a quiet place, and get relaxed. Try to recall a time when you strongly felt intense disapproval over something you observed, a time in which you felt entirely justified or righteous in that feeling. (For example, you may think of someone committing what you perceive to be a reprehensible crime or personally offensive act.) Imagine the scene in as much detail as you can. Capture this scene in the box marked "Scene 1" below, through writing and/or sketching.

2. See if you can conjure up to four other scenes (real or imagined), which also elicit strong feelings of righteous disapproval—again, in as much detail as you can. Take some time to render each of these scenes in a drawing or a piece of creative writing, as you did with scene 1.

3. Then give a name to each of your scenes, and enter them into the table below.

4. Examine each scene you have listed, and one at a time see if you can describe the source of your distress, the *why* of your disapproval. Put this into the second column opposite the appropriate scene name.

5. This entry into column B should give you a good clue about the value underlying your response. Write that in the final column. For example, perhaps you feel enraged thinking about capital punishment (column A)—because you believe any form of taking life is a sin (column B), meaning you value life and perhaps also forgiveness (column C).

Scene 1:

Scene 2:

Scene 3:

Scene 4:

Scene 5:

"Line-Crossing" Scene	Source of Distress	Value(s) Implied
1.		
2.		
3.		
4.		
5.		

Feelings connected with line-crossing moments tend to be judging feelings. There's nothing wrong with experiencing such feelings; all humans have them. They only become harmful when we fail to recognize them in ourselves and instead project them on to others. These strong feelings do give us clues to our values—which are different for different people. Most of us tend to experience values as absolute truth, but they really do fall in the category of belief systems, which can vary widely among different cultures and social networks, and they also sometimes change over time as cultures evolve. I will not spend time here trying to talk you out of your beliefs; I know they are strong. On the contrary, I appreciate that values make up some of the unique ingredients that make you who you are. You will find a better fit if you look for job in a setting where your values are well matched to your employers.

That said, feelings related to values tend to be pretty strong. You might feel enraged or horrified by something you observe or even imagine, and you may find yourself wanting to employ "should" language when talking about your values. Take note when you find yourself saying:

- "I'd never do that!"
- "It's just not me!"
- "I intensely disapprove of that."
- "That's an abomination or a sin or a crime."

Once you get in touch with feelings like these, stories and scenes may automatically come to mind. You might imagine, for example,

- a scene in which a mother is spanking her child in a grocery store;
- a childhood memory of being embarrassed or humiliated by a teacher;
- seeing intoxicated people, or simply seeing a bottle of alcohol on a shelf; or
- a newspaper article about mistreatment of a marginalized group.

Notice that one or more of these may not bother you at all. Some may evoke mild disagreement. Only concern yourself with images and scenes that evoke a strong emotional response. Those values that are most important in defining who we are will invariably be connected with the most intense emotional responses. Using art materials to further deepen and enrich these images brings us closer to understanding. The more detail and specificity, the more you have to explore and learn from.

After fully exploring these stories and scenes (starting with the feelings), you are then ready to engage the intellect by examining each item, one at a time, and discerning the meaning in it. A useful next question (answered in the second column in the table found on the last page of Exercise 8 above) is, "What is at the root of my strong feelings about this?" The answer will lead to a clearer sense of the specific value implied.

Let us look at the example of the image of a person abusing alcohol. Many people may find the image unpalatable, but perhaps for different reasons. You need to know your reasons. One person's strong response may be rooted in a fear of losing control, implying that personal control or agency is something that person values. Another may see the image as one of polluting the body with an unwanted, unhealthy substance; for this person, the predominant value may be robust physical health. Still another may be plagued by memories of an alcoholic parent and experience the image as a precursor to violent behavior, or one that symbolizes shirking of family responsibilities. So, the value may be peace and harmony or responsibility to family, respectively.

As each value becomes clear, it can be noted in the worksheet's final column. In the end, a concise list of values will begin to emerge. This serves as a useful guide in a search for a meaningful vocation, job, or career. It can increase your ability to recognize shared values and also shape the kinds of questions you might choose to ask in interviews. At the very least, the increased awareness can enable an informed decision about how far you might be willing to compromise your values in a work situation.

Below, I have included an example of a completed values chart. Remember, values are highly individualized, and these examples may not apply to you at all. Moreover, the line-crossing statements are not intended to offend. Remember, values are rooted in judgments. That said, I recommend reframing the language when it comes to naming values, emphasizing the beneficial roles they play in your sense of self. In the example below, you see a person who values care and respect for children, robust physical health and well-being, neatness, cleanliness, church, and making a good first impression. Does this give you some sense of what this person may be like? Does it conjure a visual image?

"Line-Crossing" Scene or Image	Source of Distress	Value(s) Implied
1. I see a young mother slapping a child in a grocery store.	"I remember when it happened to me - the pain + humiliation; wanting love."	Care and respect for children and their feelings.
2. Drunk man passed out on the street.	"I could never do that to my body."	Respect for body and health.
3. Teenager came to church in dirty, cutoff jeans.	"I wouldn't dress like that in my own home!"	Neatness and cleanliness. Respect for church.
4. Sloppily - written resume.	"Makes me nuts!" Such an impt document - no excuse for it!"	Neatness Good first impressions

Figure 3. Values assessment example

Interests and Talents

By this stage in the process, after thoroughly examining dissonant voices and line-crossing moments, you may be ready to indulge in exploring what I call moments of bliss. Just as line-crossing moments can teach us about our limits and values, moments of bliss can help us to realize what our soul yearns for, and thereby help us to define what work best suits us.

In the introductory chapter, I began to address what I mean by bliss. To elaborate further, in a moment of bliss, I am filled with a sense of doing what I was intended to do. Often, it is joyous—but not necessarily so. A moment of intense sorrow can also call forth deep feelings of fulfilling a purpose.

Sadly, many of us become weighed down with routines and habitual responsibilities in adulthood and go for long periods of time without the pleasure of knowing bliss. Sometimes we have to dig deep to retrieve memories of blissful moments. Many such moments first reveal themselves in childhood.

For me, moments of bliss tend to come on the heels of creative impulses. I have experienced such moments as meditative states, characterized by a feeling of time standing still. Athletes and musicians sometimes refer to the experience of being "in the zone." When writing this book, for example, I typed at my computer obsessively and energetically late into the night, even though I am by nature a morning person and ordinarily run out of steam early in the evening (especially after chasing four toddlers around all day, which coincided with the writing of the first edition of this book). The settling in after the flurry is an important part of the experience for me as well. I take time to reread and polish a piece of writing, stare at a piece of artwork, or listen at length to a completed composition.

In ushering forth memories of bliss-filled moments, I urge people to explore whatever areas in their lives are most filled with passion, no matter how irrelevant they may seem to the world of work. It has been my observation that many people retrieve their memories of bliss most readily not so much from previous work roles as from their personal lives. One may connect the memories of a wedding day with a feeling of bliss, for example. This may not apply to everyone's experience of a wedding day, but when the day is filled with blissful feelings, this sort of memory can offer keen insights about ourselves—about our passions, values, and talents. The ability to form commitments and to care for others, the need for acceptance and mutual love and respect, the valuing of family and of ritual, and perhaps a special talent for public speaking, planning, or entertaining might all underlie the bliss that a wedding day might arouse.

The interests and talents exercise below mirrors the values exercise, in that we begin with feelings and later engage the intellect. But rather than line-crossing feelings, blissful feelings are examined. The process involves (1) imagining the feeling state of bliss; (2) recalling or imagining scenes that might accompany such a feeling; and finally (3) exploring each scene in detail. In the detailed exploration, one engages the intellect to examine the "who, what and where" of the images.

Once again, I will include a fictitious example immediately following the worksheet.

Exercise 9: Clarifying Interests and Talents

1. Think of 3–5 moments in your life that could be described as "bliss-filled"; moments when you felt as though you were doing or being what you were meant to do or be, fulfilling your intended purpose. Each example may have been a peak experience that made you feel "high on life" or any poignant moment in which you truly felt you were being yourself. The moments need not pertain to employment; free your mind to open to any experience at all.

2. Write a line or two summarizing each experience at the top of each page. Then, in the space remaining, detail each experience by writing the story and sharing images or other thoughts connected with it. Be as detailed as you can.

3. Finally, examine each moment of bliss to find what it has to teach you about yourself—namely, your interests and talents. They may be stated directly, or implied. This requires some careful thought. A partner, perhaps an art therapist, may help you see things you might otherwise have blinders to.

Bliss-Filled Moment 1:

Exercise 9: Clarifying Interests and Talents (continued)

Bliss-Filled Moment 2:

Bliss-Filled Moment 3:

Bliss-Filled Moment 4:

Exercise 9: Clarifying Interests and Talents (continued)

Bliss-Filled Moment 5:

"Moment of Bliss"	Interests Implied	Talents Implied
1.		
2.		
3.		
4.		
5.		

Let us take a closer look at an example of exercise 9.

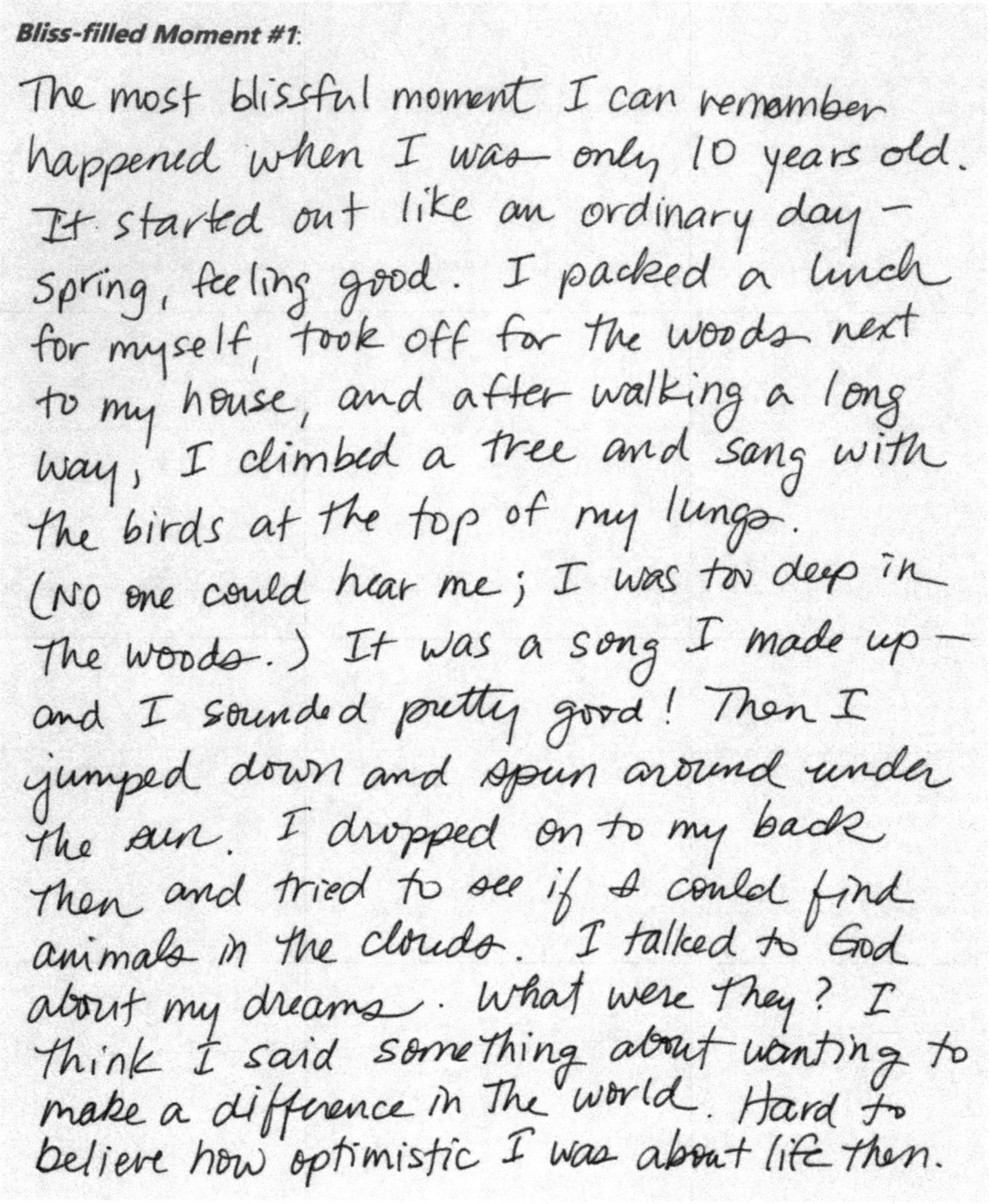

Bliss-filled Moment #1:

The most blissful moment I can remember happened when I was only 10 years old. It started out like an ordinary day — Spring, feeling good. I packed a lunch for myself, took off for the woods next to my house, and after walking a long way, I climbed a tree and sang with the birds at the top of my lungs. (No one could hear me; I was too deep in the woods.) It was a song I made up — and I sounded pretty good! Then I jumped down and spun around under the sun. I dropped on to my back then and tried to see if I could find animals in the clouds. I talked to God about my dreams. What were they? I think I said something about wanting to make a difference in the world. Hard to believe how optimistic I was about life then.

Figure 4. Example of a bliss-filled moment

Examining the example above, I am reminded of how magical youth can be. Sometimes if people cannot recall blissful moments, I refer them to childhood to see if any useful images emerge.

What do we learn about the young girl in this single example? I will list a few observations, in consecutive order—not necessarily in order of importance.

- This is someone who is clearly drawn to and nourished by the outdoors.
- She is resourceful and possesses an independent spirit. (She retreated to the woods alone, packed her own lunch.)

- She very likely has some musical talent as a singer and has a creative bent. (She made up her own song).
- She appears to be more introverted than extroverted. (She is relieved that no one can hear her singing, enjoys her own company, and basks in the solitude.)
- This is also a spiritually oriented person with a perceived calling, a mission, a lofty and worthy purpose. (She dreams of making a difference in the world.)
- She recalls this event with nostalgia; we wonder if she has lost touch with her youthful, ambitious spirit.

We may deduce from these notes that, with respect to her talents, even at a young age, this individual showed some musical ability. (We usually love what we are good at.) She is resourceful, able to manage tasks independently, and quick to show initiative. She appears to be strongly influenced by her environment, and she has revealed some interests as well (the outdoors, music, spirituality). She strikes me also as being a high achiever, holding high standards and high expectations for herself.

Letting Images Emerge

There is wisdom in dreams—daydreams as well as night dreams—and unless we pursue them directly, imaginatively, and courageously, we may never access them, and we will certainly never realize them.

"Allowing an image to emerge" is McAuliffe's third stage in the career exploration process (1993, 36), after "acknowledging dissonant voices" and "pausing to assess." An image or images of self-fulfillment, of a "dream job," may emerge spontaneously if we are open to the arrival and feel worthy of the dream. Some of the exercises in this book might help to coax them out. They may also be called forth through guided imagery.

Following is a guided-imagery text that has been useful to me in career-life planning workshops I have delivered. Like most guided imagery, it works best when spoken slowly in a clear and calm voice, over soft music or a very soft drumbeat. The background sound creates a holding environment that helps to contain and preserve the sacredness of the space, making it safer for images to emerge. I believe it is helpful, too, for the facilitator to keep his or her intuitive abilities sharp and to ad lib on the basic script offered here based on this intuition, in order to respond effectively to the needs of the particular group or individual being guided.

Following the guided imagery, I allow plenty of time for people to record their impressions in visual images, adding words as they seem appropriate.

Exercise 10: Magic Carpet Ride Guided Meditation

Find a comfortable place and position, ideally lying on your back. If you prefer, you may also sit on a cushion or on a chair in a manner that allows you to relax and yet remain alert and able to breathe easily, with feet flat on the ground and back straight. Follow the instructions of the person reading the progressive relaxation and guided-imagery script.

Be sure to assume a receptive posture. Prepare for mystery, surprise, even confusion. Do not try to *make* images; rather, let them reveal themselves to you as they will. Approach the process with childlike interest, wonder, and curiosity. Be open to whatever comes and whatever it has to teach.

Script:

Close your eyes, so that you can open your mind's eye to the imaginal space that surrounds you. Take a deep breath through your nose, exhaling slowly through your mouth. Then a second, then a third. Then simply allow the breath to flow in and out, gently and naturally.

As you begin to relax, attend to any parts of your body that might be holding tension. Find those places, and systematically tense them, hold and release. Begin with your toes. Tense. Hold. And release. Move to your calves and your thighs. Feel the tension in your abdomen, your diaphragm. Tense. Hold. And release.

Find any tension that your fingers or hands might be holding. Clench your fists, your forearms; hold and release. Find the tension in your shoulders and your neck. Tense. Hold. Release. Locate any tension in your face, your forehead, or your eyes. Tense. Hold. Release. And breathe.

Now feel or imagine your body lying on the floor. Feel along your back as the fibers of a magic carpet begin to weave themselves beneath you. Notice the texture and feel of the fibers, and watch as the colors begin to reveal themselves. (Remember, you are seeing with your mind's eye, so there is no need to move your head.) Know that the carpet forming beneath you is a magic carpet, strong and fully able to hold your weight, regardless of the density and texture of the fibers. Take some time to notice the carpet in all its glorious detail: the colors, textures, shapes, designs.

As you lie on the floor, watch with your mind's eye as a tiny spot of sunlight opens in the ceiling above you—slowly opening, little by little, until the ceiling dissolves. In time the walls, too, begin to dissolve around you. Finally, even the floor dissolves away, and you are left suspended by the strength of the carpet on which you lie. Then the carpet begins to tremble, ready to rise and take you on a journey to your future.

Enjoy the ride as the carpet rises above surrounding trees and buildings, over the city or town or countryside from whence you began.

Note the sights below as you travel from this place to a place five years into your future. Pay close attention to where the carpet is taking you; notice the speed with which you are traveling, the distance traveled, and the geography of the landscape.

After a time, you experience a sensation of slowly spiraling downward. You may not be able to see the ground clearly, but you will know when you have landed. Then, feel a new floor forming beneath you, walls rising around you, and a ceiling forming above you, all of it being put together in the same manner in which your former shelter disassembled itself.

When the space around you has become fully assembled, and when you feel ready, bring your attention to two doors in the room. One is a door you might recognize. It is the door to your future. Behind it lie the places, people, and things you anticipate in the coming years—five years from now. The other door is a mysterious one. You did not expect it. You have no idea what lies behind this door. Take some time to regard the exteriors of both doors, for in a few minutes you will be asked to choose one of the doors as you continue your journey.

When you are ready, get up from your carpet, choose one of the doors in the room, and walk over to it. Will it be the familiar door or the mystery door? Take another deep breath. Open the door you have chosen. Enter the space behind it.

What sights greet you here? Take in the place with all your senses. Is it warm or cold? What can you smell? What does the floor feel like? Notice any furnishings, objects, colors, textures, and items on the walls.

Take in every detail. Walk around and browse through the items. Investigate the items you see. Is there a window? If you find one, look out to see what may be on the other side. Are there people here? Who are they? Talk with them to see if they can tell you more about this place.

Before you leave this place, take one last sweeping look around and promise yourself that you will remember every detail. Then say goodbye and walk out the door you entered. See your magic carpet lying before you, waiting for you. Take your time lying down again, and make yourself comfortable.

Now, as before, watch a tiny spot of light appear in the ceiling above you. See the ceiling dissolve, the walls, and finally the floor beneath you. Surrender yourself to the strong carpet as it gathers energy and rises up, up into the sky once more, spiraling into the air, carrying you back effortlessly along the same path that brought you here.

Before you know it, you find yourself back in the city, town, or countryside from whence you began, lying comfortably on your magic carpet, and then on the bare floor.

When you are ready, take three more deep breaths, and slowly open your eyes. Find your paper and something to draw with so you may record your impressions.

Record your impressions in the spaces provided below.

Perhaps the most compelling thing about this exercise is the enormous variety of impressions it elicits from people. Each person's individuality shines, and the input of others and their observations can greatly enrich the images that emerge. My approach to interpreting the content does not include assigning particular meanings to particular symbols; rather, I let the images speak for themselves and enter into dialogue with them, in the tradition of Shaun McNiff (1988) and Paolo Knill (1995).

The intent of this guided-imagery exercise, as with all the exercises introduced in this exploratory stage, is to bring forth richness, stir the soup, and uncover the many aspects that make us individuals, particularly those that bring us joy. Imagine, sketch, and write everything down. Once surrounded by the various images, once you're swimming in the soup, you will find that the cream will rise to the top. The most essential aspects of you and your dominant qualities will weed themselves out and present themselves. They will demand the most attention. Your job is to grapple with them, to clarify them for yourself, and finally to put them forward in both written and verbal presentations. A key holder of this essence of you is your professional portfolio—in particular, your résumé. Step 5 will walk you through this process.

GIVING SUBSTANCE TO IMAGES

The job you seek isn't out there in some job description;
it's already inside you, aching to get out.
—John Tarnoff, *Boomer Reinvention: How to Create Your Dream Career over 50*

Once you have a good sense of who you are and what you have to offer in the way of work in the world, you need to find ways to communicate that to others, in order to facilitate an appropriate match with a position that suits you. Some key documents come into play here.

Professional Portfolios and the Art of Résumé Writing

A professional portfolio is your personal collection of job-related application materials. Generally, the portfolio will include a résumé, lists of professional references and letters of recommendation, sometimes transcripts and copies of pertinent licenses. The professional portfolio may also include writing samples and samples of professional work done in graphic design or other artistic modalities, perhaps a formal statement of intent or a teaching philosophy. People seeking consulting jobs may also need a statement of purpose, proof of malpractice insurance, and a professional disclosure statement.

Often people use the term *CV* (curriculum vita) interchangeably with the term *résumé*; these are actually different documents, with a curriculum vita being used more for academic positions and also being much lengthier, as the CV will typically include lists of courses taught, scholarly publications, professional presentations, and so forth. Even for a person needing a curriculum vita, I advocate a straightforward one- or two-page résumé, a summary that can be read or scanned quickly, with more detailed documentation attached.

A résumé is key, a crucial tool for anyone conducting a job search. Even if the job you apply for does not require one, I strongly recommend having one. You can personalize and tailor a résumé so that it accurately conveys the essence of you in a way that a completed application form can never do. The process of writing a résumé can itself be enlightening and affirming, and it can optimize career success.

People today generally want more than just a job. Don't you? Wouldn't you prefer meaningful and satisfying work that feels good for the soul? Don't you want bliss? You are more likely to achieve it by crafting a highly individualized résumé designed to attract quality (not quantity) contacts and interviews. A good résumé draws the right people to you.

This task calls for something other than the traditional, formulaic "just fill out this template" approach. I approach résumé-writing as an art. As a résumé artist (to coin a term), I sift through the variety of material and images gleaned from self-exploratory processes (like the ones presented here), introspection and dialogue. I allow dominant qualities to emerge, and I engage a creative process so that I may clearly and concisely present an image that effectively conveys the unique essence of a person. The material is shaped with whatever format, text, and paper stock best express a person's qualities.

A highly individualized résumé stands out from the cookie-cutter variety and leaves a strong and memorable impression. No two finished products will be exactly alike, just as no two individuals are exactly alike. People are naturally attracted to a résumé that accurately reflects a person's essence. The better your interests and values match the reader of your résumé, the stronger the attraction.

Of course, when you narrow your focus, you narrow your options. Therefore, not everyone will feel the same degree of attraction to your résumé or fully appreciate your style or your unique blend of talents and attributes. But remember, the objective is quality of match, not quantity of offers. If you are like most people, you only need one job, and it may as well be the right job.

I am reminded of an artistically inclined individual who chose to locate his text flush to the right of the page (see the fictionalized example, figure 5, below). He found that "artsy" friends loved his résumé. However, he did encounter one person who did not respond favorably to it. When I inquired about that reader, he shared that he had little in common with the gentleman, a "linear-minded," conservative fellow who found the résumé "just too hard to read." Not surprisingly, this man was not a person with whom my client could see himself working anyway.

Let me pause a moment to reflect upon the examples included in this manual. While I do think it can be helpful to share specific examples and excerpts from résumés to illustrate some points, these are not intended to be templates suitable for copying. Certainly, you may adopt features that resonate with you, but strive to represent that unique picture of the essence of you.

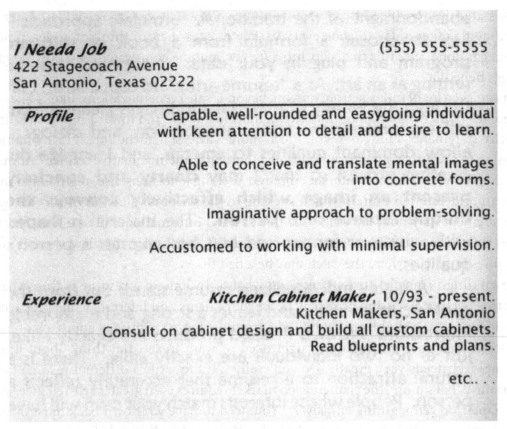

I Needa Job
422 Stagecoach Avenue
San Antonio, Texas 02222

(555) 555-5555

Profile	Capable, well-rounded and easygoing individual with keen attention to detail and desire to learn.

Able to conceive and translate mental images into concrete forms.

Imaginative approach to problem-solving.

Accustomed to working with minimal supervision. |
| *Experience* | ***Kitchen Cabinet Maker***, 10/93 - present. Kitchen Makers, San Antonio Consult on cabinet design and build all custom cabinets. Read blueprints and plans.

etc.. . . |

Figure 5. Flush-right-margin résumé example

Some minimal standards must be adhered to in order to make every résumé readable and accessible, to make each one as easy to take in as possible while still maintaining individuality. Résumés must be neatly printed, with no errors or misspellings, on résumé-quality paper. I recommend twenty-four- to thirty-two-pound bond paper, a heavier weight paper than the more familiar twenty-pound printer paper. The heavier weight provides a more substantial feel and greater durability and displays color better.

I have yet to find a person whose essence cannot be eloquently summarized in a single page (with additional detail attached in clearly organized pages, as appropriate). An elegant one-page summary is easily digested at a glance, with all critical information included, and one does not risk "losing" important messages on additional pages. Beyond these basic parameters, there is a great deal of room to be creative.

In order to fully and accurately convey who you are, on paper as well as in person, I encourage you to stick your neck out and take stands on issues that resonate with you and your values, to move beyond a mere listing of sterile tasks and abilities, and to let your personality shine through. If you feel as though you do not know yourself well enough to do so (as many who have lived their lives for others will confess), take time to do some self-reflection to uncover those gems, preferably with a competent therapist or professional coach. It may be interesting to review the scene from the 1999 film *Runaway Bride,* where the character Maggie, played by Julia Roberts, realizes she lacks even the most basic understanding of her own likes and desires. (See https://www.youtube.com/watch?v=KqyGc7-UEj4.) Later in the movie, Maggie takes a day to cook every variety of eggs she can think of, to learn how she likes her eggs done. (See this final clip, https://www.youtube.com/watch?v=ciLfnJAkvgk.) She liked eggs benedict.

You can get a lot of mileage from moving beyond "safe" generalizations, like "I like to work with people" (which is tantamount to saying nothing at all) and toward more revealing and descriptive statements. One can reveal much more with a statement like, "I bring humor and compassion to my nursing practice, and I am a thorough and imaginative trainer." Admittedly, should this nurse's path encounter an employer seeking a no-nonsense, regimented nurse to work in an understaffed unit, in which sticking to the script is valued in in-service trainers, such a statement may not play well. I see this as good information, not as a loss. Neither set of values is necessarily bad or wrong, but they are different, and in my view, there is no sense casting lines in places where the catch may be a bad fit.

The guiding principle I use in deciding what to include in a résumé is this: what truly defines this person? Focusing primarily upon your talents and interests while preparing this critical document is a slightly different twist from the more traditional approach of focusing on what one imagines an employer might need or want to see. But think about it; on one hand, employer needs vary greatly. Do you really want to write a different résumé for every application? What's more, the changing job market requires even greater self-reliance, as noted in the chapter on reimagining employers. You need to have your own back most of all—not only for your own sake but as a steward of what the world really needs from you.

This principle guides not only the choice of résumé content but also the way in which the content is presented, the style. An artistic eye can help to shape the emotional impact of a résumé. Why does this matter? It is my contention, regardless of how objective people may try to be, that for most employers, hiring is ultimately an emotional decision, not a logical one. People hire people, not pieces of paper or abstract lists of skills, and they hire people they like, people with whom they feel comfortable. If someone likes you enough, he or she will find a way to justify the hiring if needed on paper. I recall applying for a job just out of college for which I was (on paper) sorely underqualified. It took some nerve to apply, but I was certain I could do the job. The interviewer liked me and wanted to hire me, and by the time she had a chance to review my paperwork thoroughly, it was too late for her to turn back. She relaxed the stated requirements in order to bring me on board.

The intense period of introspection and the process of articulating talents and interests in a résumé have clear therapeutic effects. Increased self-awareness is an important by-product, and with it comes a heightened confidence and optimism for realizing goals. Both are necessary for negotiating in today's job market, where self-reliance is required, as is the ability to envision niches amid the ever-changing scenery.

It has been my experience that the qualities of self-awareness, confidence, and optimism, which the résumé-writing process can nurture, may be even more important to an effective job search than the résumé itself. I remember working with a woman I'll call Yael. During our initial consultation, she shared that she had really wanted to leave her current job for a couple of years, but she had never put much effort into a search. After her résumé was completed, I phoned Yael to arrange for her to pick up the finished copy. Excitedly, she shared that she had landed a new job that very day. Bolstered and energized by the résumé-writing process, and armed with a clearer sense of herself and her skills, she had called upon a company to inquire about a particular opening and was offered a position right over the phone.

Because effective résumé writing requires artistic talents as well as technical skills, and because another person can often bring a fresh and unbiased perspective on a person's best traits—absent the doubting and critical voices that sometimes accompany self-assessments—it can be a wise choice to seek professional help from a résumé artist. To be sure, most people can fill in the blanks of an application form; this is a purely technical task. But not everyone can bring an artist's intuition to the crafting of a résumé, just as it would be rare for a CEO to prepare his own corporate marketing materials. (CEOs routinely hire artists and consultants for such tasks, while of course remaining involved in the process by describing the image they wish to convey.) A résumé artist can also help you to see and appreciate talents and uncover interests you may have not mustered the courage to confront or embrace.

Gathering Data

The first step in writing a résumé is to gather information—as much as possible. In addition to the worksheets already completed, I suggest gathering data about experience, education, and achievements in a worksheet like the one included on the following pages. Later, with all this data in front of us, we can sift through for the best gems to include in the résumé itself.

The following worksheet is not a résumé template or outline. Rather, it serves as a vehicle to aid in the collection of information that will later be reviewed and reorganized to present the candidate in the most accurate and flattering manner possible. For the finished résumé, some information will necessarily be cut, abbreviated, or modified, and most will be rearranged to best reflect individual strengths.

While filling in the blanks, keep in mind that the process of writing a résumé is itself of value, because it helps to inventory abilities, build confidence, and of course to help jog your memory of all those dates, names, and places that can be hard to recall. In this way, the worksheet can also serve as a cheat sheet when you complete application forms.

For the section on describing job duties, refer to the Action Word list that follows the worksheet. Get in the habit of using action words to describe duties and achievements. Begin every phrase with an action verb, and then follow with a subject (e.g., handled mail, counseled people with disabilities, negotiated contracts, wrote three successful grants, designed an afterschool program, increased annual sales by 20 percent, set up a database for customer tracking, etc.). Use present tense for a current job (e.g., maintain books, supervise twenty-five support staff, etc.). Be thorough, and print clearly.

Exercise 11: Résumé-Writing Worksheet

Make the information on this worksheet thorough and complete. Save it as a lasting resource; update it as the years pass. Use the information as a menu from which to create a unique résumé for each job you seek.

Name: _____ Date updated: _____

I. Personal Information

Address: _____
City: _____ State: _____ Zip: _____
Phone: (_____) _____ Email: _____
Permanent address (if different): _____
City: _____ State: _____ Zip: _____
Phone: (_____) _____ Email: _____

If you anticipate ever requesting a security clearance, you may need to record every place you have ever resided. You may also be required to identify and locate roommates, so record that here too!

_____
_____
_____

II. Education

First college or university: _____
Location: _____ State: _____
Degree: _____
Major(s): _____ Minor(s): _____
Date obtained: _____ Major GPA: _____ Overall GPA: _____

Other college or university: _____
Location: _____ State: _____
Degree: _____
Major(s): _____ Minor(s): _____
Date obtained: _____ Major GPA: _____ Overall GPA: _____
Other schools attended (except high school), training or certifications received, licenses obtained:

_____
_____
_____

_____

_____

III. Experience Information (Consider all experience—paid, unpaid, volunteer—most recent first.)

(Duplicate this template as needed to include other positions.)

Position title 1: _____(PT) (FT) (Intern) (Volunteer)
Organization name: _____
Address: _____
City:_____ State: _____
Dates employed (months & years only) From: _____ To: _____
Name of supervisor(s): _____
Duties and responsibilities: _____

_____

_____

Personal attributes you found important and used successfully in this position:

_____

_____

Specific performance accomplishments or contributions you made to this job:

_____

_____

_____

_____

Position title 2: _____(PT) (FT) (Intern) (Volunteer)
Organization name: _____
Address: _____
City:_____ State: _____
Dates employed (months & years only) From: _____ To: _____
Name of supervisor(s): _____
Duties and responsibilities: _____

_____

_____

_____

Personal attributes you found important and used successfully in this position:

_____

_____
_____
_____
_____

Specific performance accomplishments or contributions you made to this job:

_____
_____
_____
_____
_____

Position title 3: _____(PT) (FT) (Intern) (Volunteer)

Organization name: _____

Address: _____

City: _____ State: _____

Dates employed (months & years only) From: _____ To: _____

Name of supervisor(s): _____

Duties and responsibilities: _____
_____
_____
_____
_____

Personal attributes you found important and used successfully in this position:

_____
_____
_____
_____

Specific performance accomplishments or contributions you made to this job:

_____
_____
_____
_____
_____

Position title 4: _____(PT) (FT) (Intern) (Volunteer)

Organization name: _____

Address: _____

City: _____ State: _____

Dates employed (months & years only) From: _____ To: _____

Name of supervisor(s): _____

Duties and responsibilities: _____

_____

_____

_____

_____

Personal attributes you found important and used successfully in this position:

_____

_____

_____

_____

_____

Specific performance accomplishments or contributions you made to this job:

_____

_____

_____

_____

_____

Position title 5: _____(PT) (FT) (Intern) (Volunteer)

Organization name: _____

Address: _____

City: _____ State: _____

Dates employed (months & years only) From: _____ To: _____

Name of supervisor(s): _____

Duties and responsibilities: _____

_____

_____

_____

_____

Personal attributes you found important and used successfully in this position:

_____

_____

_____

_____

Specific performance accomplishments or contributions you made to this job:

_____

_____

_____

_____

IV. Special Strengths and Competencies

Write your special talents, skills, training, languages (e.g., artistic skills, computer skills, special licenses), etc.:

_____

_____

_____

_____

_____

_____

_____

V. Other

1. Memberships in professional associations, clubs, community groups, or volunteer and religious organizations. Include the name of the association, offices held, and the dates. Add any significant activities attributed to your leadership:

_____

_____

_____

2. Awards and Honors (e.g., academic, athletic, social, civic, or any scholarship not based on financial need): _____

_____

_____

3. Creative professional activities (e.g., articles written, inventions, projects presented or displayed):

_____

_____

_____

_____

VI. Personal References

List references on a separate page, not on your résumé. Avoid using relatives. Generally, three or four professional or academic references and one personal reference will be sufficient. Be sure to get permission from any reference before using his or her name! Send each a thank-you note for volunteering to help you, and keep them informed on your job search progress.

1. Name: _____ Phone: (_____) _____
Address: _____ City: _____ State: _____
Position: _____

2. Name: _____ Phone: (_____) _____
   Address: _____ City: _____ State: _____
   Position: _____

3. Name: _____ Phone: (_____) _____
   Address: _____ City: _____ State: _____
   Position: _____

4. Name: _____ Phone: (_____) _____
   Address: _____ City: _____ State: _____
   Position: _____

VII. Anything else worth noting that helps to define you as a person.

_____

_____

_____

_____

1. Put this worksheet onto a computer file and keep it for future use.
2. Consider the sample résumé formats and start to build your résumé.
3. Update your résumé worksheet annually. Go through the past year and consider your experiences and accomplishments, recording them while they are fresh in your mind.

achieved	created	followed	memorized	reproduced
accepted	cut	formulated	mentored	resolved
acted	dealt with	found	met	responded
addressed	debated	founded	modeled	retained
adjusted	decided	gained	monitored	retrained
advised	defined	gathered	motivated	retrieved
aided	delivered	gave	negotiated	reviewed
allocated	designed	generated	nursed	scheduled
anticipated	detected	graphed	nurtured	screened
applied	determined	guided	observed	searched
appraised	developed	handled	obtained	selected
arranged	devised	helped	operated	serviced
assembled	diagnosed	hired	ordered	set up
assessed	directed	hosted	organized	sketched
attained	discovered	identified	persuaded	simplified
balanced	dispatched	illustrated	painted	sold
briefed	displayed	imagined	performed	solved
brought	distributed	improved	placed	sorted
budgeted	drafted	improvised	planned	sought
built	drew	increased	played	specialized
calculated	drove	influenced	possessed	spoke
cared for	duplicated	initiated	posted	studied
carried	edited	inspected	prepared	summarized
chaired	eliminated	inspired	prescribed	supplied
charted	empathized	instituted	presented	surveyed
checked	emphasized	instructed	produced	taught
clarified	employed	interviewed	promoted	tended
classified	encouraged	intuited	proofread	tested
cleaned	enforced	invented	protected	took
coached	enjoyed	inventoried	publicized	trained
collaborated	entered	investigated	purchased	transcribed
collated	estimated	judged	raised	traveled
collected	exceeded	kept	read	treated
completed	excelled	learned	received	tutored
conceived	executed	led	recognized	understood
conducted	expanded	lifted	recorded	updated
confronted	expressed	listened	recruited	upgraded
conserved	extracted	loaded	redesigned	used
contacted	facilitated	made	reduced	utilized
copied	farmed	maintained	referred	weighed
corrected	figured	managed	renewed	won
counseled	filed	mapped	repaired	worked
counted	focused	mastered	reported	wrote

Figure 6. Action words

Résumé Anatomy

A résumé need not correspond to any particular format, so job seekers are at liberty to include whatever information seems most relevant and to downplay or even omit certain items and highlight others. But the résumé does need to summarize in a concise manner any and all information pertinent to your ability, qualifications, and working style. In other words, it needs to answer the question, "Who are you, and why should I hire you?" Two essential parts form the backbone to a résumé to answer these two questions.

The Profile: First, a profile, or a summary of skills, abilities, and attributes, encompasses the essence of a person, including dominant qualities that emerge from material pulled from self-awareness exercises and in dialogue with a résumé artist. Brevity is important here, and bulleted items are easiest to read quickly. Studies in perception have shown that the human brain can easily hold no more than five bits of data at a time; this is a rough guideline I use for how many items to include on a profile, though it is by no means set in stone.

The Evidence: Once this essence is summarized, the remainder of the résumé offers support for the statements made in the profile. This evidence can be summarized in a variety of sections. The order in which you list your supporting statements depends upon what you want to emphasize more or less, but for the most part the sections will include some version of the following:

- employment or work history
- education and training
- licenses, certifications, memberships, and professional affiliations
- any other pertinent information that does not fit into these areas

Additional support comes from people who know you. The names, addresses and phone numbers of references, who are people who can vouch for your strengths, are generally not listed on the résumé itself. However, most add a line at the end of the résumé stating something like "References furnished upon request," or to be more thorough, "References and portfolio furnished upon request" or "References and writing samples furnished upon request." The particular statement depends on what you want to make available from your portfolio. The final line also serves as a sort of signal that the reader has reached the end of the résumé.

The Objective: What about an objective? I often hear this question as a worried inquiry, sometimes with a gasp. It is a fact that many, many résumé templates begin with a bold announcement inviting this piece. My unwavering opinion on this subject: objectives are important to state and to be clear about, but they belong in a cover letter, not on a résumé. When I see them on résumés, they typically are written in such a general fashion that they lack meaning (e.g., "I am seeking a job that will utilize my skills and give me an opportunity to advance"), or else they are written so specifically that they effectively rule out golden opportunities that a person may not have imagined. Especially in today's market, with jobs and entire industries becoming obsolete every day, it is important to remain flexible to the variety of opportunities that can arise. Besides, why waste prime space on a résumé with ambiguous statements?

Let us turn to the second main part of the résumé: information intended to provide evidence or support for one's profile. While we must be selective here, I have found it most valuable to first collect all the pertinent data and then to discern the essentials to include. The résumé worksheet and exercises above are intended to help with that initial gathering of data.

Many people have the misconception that if they have more than one area of interest or talent, they need to create more than one résumé to address each area and to use different résumés to apply to different types of work. In a wholeness-based approach to résumé writing like the one advocated here, the goal is to give the reader a complete picture of what the person has to offer, leaving no stone unturned. Indeed, a prospective employer may find a seemingly "unrelated" talent or interest intriguing or at least find the person well rounded or interesting in ways he or she may not have anticipated. One résumé is enough. The art lies in conveying that essence as a cohesive image.

Let me share an example that pertains here. A person I'll call David came to me seeking career counseling and brought with him a two-page résumé that reflected only one dimension of his background, his sales experience. He began the résumé with a general objective, which consumed about an eighth of the page, listed a few sales skills and summarized a few sales jobs from his employment history. It was typical of many résumés I see.

David had two other major areas of interest, which were nowhere reflected in his résumé. One of his omissions was his "secret life" as a musician. He was a consummate and accomplished guitarist who practiced his instrument several hours a day and studied with some of the finest musicians in his city, though he had never performed in public. The other omission was a love for the restaurant industry. The bulk of the restaurant experience dated back to his college years.

First off, I insisted that David, for homework, arrange to perform at an open mic session in his city. (The first priority, in my view, was to feed this neglected passion.) Then I worked on introducing a better sense of David's essence into his résumé. An abbreviated excerpt of that résumé appears on the following page.

David Fender

101 Reggae Street ♥ New York, New York, 10001
(555) 555-5555 ♥ davidfender@yahoo.com

Profile

- ♥ Disciplined, versatile and self-directed high achiever.
- ♥ Outstanding track record in sales and management.
- ♥ Well-developed consultative selling, closing and communication skills.
- ♥ Knowledge and experience in all aspects of the restaurant industry.
- ♥ Effective and creative planner with an keen eye for cost reduction strategies.
- ♥ Versatile guitarist with special interest in jazz and jazz blues.

Employment

- ♥ **District Sales Manager**, 6/92 – 10/93.
  Data R Us, Harvard Satellite Office, New Hampshire
  Advanced from temporary position in finance. Engaged in all aspects of prospecting, sales and closing.

- ♥ **Salesperson** (twice rated #2 in company), 10/90 – 5/92
  Fox Industries, Portland, Maine
  Handled proposals, demonstrations and closings. Sold over $100K in three months.

- ♥ **Function Coordinator**, 12/86 – 8/90
  Famous Restaurant, San Diego, California
  Performed sales and staffing responsibilities. Organized large functions. Transferred to Chicago to open a premier steakhouse for the company. Assisted new management in scheduling and training staff.

  [...]

Education

- ♥ Berklee College of Music, Boston, Massachusetts, 6/79 – 5/81
  Completed studies in arranging, theory, harmony and professional film scoring.

References furnished upon request.

Figure 7. Excerpt of David's résumé *after*

Once we finished the résumé, David and I knew that one of three responses could be expected from potential employers:

- One reader might dislike the résumé and respond with, "What do I care that he's a musician?" Given David's insecurity about performing, a derisive attitude was the last thing he needed.
- A second reader, from her employer perspective, might not have any particular interest in musical skills or restaurant knowledge, but she might find the applicant more interesting and well rounded, and she may even share an interest in music that could enable a point of mutual appreciation beyond the sales position in question.
- A third might actually seek an applicant with all David's talents. (Imagine that.)

Fortunately for David, within a matter of a few weeks, he landed something of a dream job. He was offered a position as an account executive supervising sales for a growing chain of restaurant/nightclubs, in which live entertainment was a major part of the fare. In this position, all his skills and interests mattered. He was perfectly suited to this work.

You may wonder what happened with David's initial homework assignment. Because the territory was untried, we had no idea where taking the risk to perform may lead. I myself had never heard David play, but I certainly sensed his passion, and I believe he needed to honor and give voice to that passion and be willing to let the chips fall where they may. At least he would better understand what it might all be about. When we stifle passion, our awareness of what it means to us can become clouded or distorted. David agreed.

By his report, the risk brought him increased clarity and a new pleasure in life. He began to find ways to perform more often. A family man, he was pleased to realize that finding time to perform did not require that he give up parts of his life for a life on the road, as some musicians do. On the contrary, he learned a number of ways in which his talent could enrich his life and the lives of others without being all consuming. He even found moments to perform at the very venue where he landed that dream job—making it even more of a dream job than he had ever previously allowed himself to dream.

Artistic Presentation and Style

You may have noticed a couple of artistic liberties I took in David's *after* résumé, above. Do you recognize the bullets? Yes, they are guitar picks. This offers a subtle way to support that important aspect of David's essence, his love of guitar playing. I also selected color and typeface that helped to convey his personality. How did I know? A résumé artist often gets a sense of these things, but I also checked it out with David. He loved his résumé and felt it really reflected him. Green is his favorite color, and the slightly fancy but still readable typeface hints at his fancy side.

Whenever I deliver a résumé-writing workshop, I like to use an exercise in which I quickly walk around the room, passing out sample résumés. As soon as I complete my circle, I retrace my steps and pick each sample up again. Then I ask people to jot down whatever impressions come to mind about the résumés they only briefly saw. I remind them that a prospective employer will form an initial impression of their résumé in only a few seconds, and this impression will determine whether they read on. What I don't tell them is that many of the résumés they have scanned are "before and after" résumés of the same people. The exercise is an excellent way to bring home to people the importance of making use of the artistic tools we have available to us to emphasize or deemphasize items and also to impart style and suggest visual images consistent with our personalities.

You can get a sense of the impact of the exercise by glancing at the examples on the following pages. What stands out to most people in figure 8 are the capitalized headings and white space. This does the job candidate no good at all. Figure 9, on the other hand, adjusts the typeface size and boldness and uses more sensible positioning to ensure the person's name will be remembered, to highlight her strengths right off the bat, and to eliminate or downplay the less important text. Both examples fit onto a single page, but look how much more the second example tells us about Rosalind. As far as content goes, we learn about her varied interests, her working style, and her community involvement. The unique typeface applied to her name better reflects her personality, with a touch of flair we would have no notion of in figure 8. Which version makes a stronger impression on you?

Rosalind T. Goldstein
17 Tulip Lane
Fictionaltown, CH 55555
(555) 555-5555

OBJECTIVE:	FULL-TIME employment, utilizing my previous experience of dealing with people.
EDUCATION:	Fictional School of Dental Nursing
EXPERIENCE:	Farley Corporation D.B.A. Helping Others (June 1, 1992 to present)

Office Manager/Patient Benefits Coordinator:

* answering phone calls
* greeting clients
* maintaining copies of clinician schedules
* ascertaining insurance benefits and confirming benefits
* fielding client questions Re: billing and benefits
* keeping medical records accessible and proper order
* word processing: Microsoft Word
* responsible for office upkeep and supplies

HELPING OTHERS, INC., (1982-1991)

Receptionist/Medical Billing/Data Entry

REFERENCES:	Available upon request

Figure 8. Rosalind *before*

Rosalind T. Goldstein

17 Tulip Lane
Fictionaltown, CH 55555

Office: (555) 444-4444
Home: (555) 555-5555

- Warm, personable and conscientious self-starter with seasoned skills in **office management, fund-raising** and **event planning/coordination**.
- Very strong people skills; able to maintain poise and rapport even when dealing with crises, "difficult" clients, children and collections problems.
- Familiar with operation of mental health and insurance agencies and small businesses.
- Long-standing interest in music and the arts.
- Computer literate; skilled in Microsoft Word, medical billing software.

Professional Experience

Office Manager/Patient Benefits Coordinator, 1992 - present
Farley Corporation, D/B/A Helping Others, Fictionaltown
Manage office. Handle special billing problems. Prepare reports, correspondence. Put clients at ease for therapy appointments. Organize staff parties. Redecorated the office.

Receptionist/Medical Billing/Data Entry, 1982 - 1991
Helping Others, Inc., Fictionaltown
Greeted clients. Screened/referred callers. Handled intakes and billing.

Manager/Bookkeeper, Ace Shoes, Metropolis, 1978 - 1982
Purchased inventory. Managed sales, personnel and bookkeeping.

Community Service

Parent Teacher Organization (PTO)
Active member/spokesperson for 10 years. Served as President and Vice President. Led successful fundraiser to build playground and school addition.

School Committee and Youth Commission, Fiction Temple
Co-chaired 25th Anniversary Art Show in 1986; participated in art show committees in prior years (solicited donations, located artists, purchased/hung art, prepared hall.)

Education

Dental Assistant certificate, Fictional School of Dental Nursing
Completed 1-year certificate training and 7 years employment as dental assistant.

References furnished upon request.

Figure 9. Rosalind *after*

Choices of paper, symbols, visual images, and even watermarks can be incorporated in subtle, even subliminal ways to help reflect the person portrayed. Jane (below) worked with contractors in the homebuilding industry. One subtle way in which she put her best foot forward was with simple house shapes (pentagons) for bullets in her profile.

Jane Doe
111 Brookside, Keene, New York 55555
(555) 555-5555

- Creative, straightforward and capable sale professional.
- Organized and detail oriented, with superb problem solving skills.
- Quick learner with demonstrated initiative and resourcefulness.
- Computer literate; familiar with CAD and 20/20.
- Extensively trained, with vast product knowledge and skills in design strategies in contracting and home remodeling.

etc...

Figure 10. Creative graphics

I have seen more dramatic touches. As a person in charge of hiring in a few different positions myself, I recall once receiving a large, three-fold résumé with a three-by-five photograph of the applicant on the front. I personally thought it a bit of overkill, and I did not choose to interview this person myself, but I can leave room for the possibility that someone else might have been sold. To the individual's credit, he did make an impression, and I have never forgotten his résumé.

The main point is to include what suits and best reflects the individual. Moreover, as résumé writers and résumé artists, we need to take care that the artistic styles we use do reflect the people portrayed and not our own personal styles.

Much can be done with typefaces. With one individual, I incorporated an ornate, flowery typeface (Sara Goodnature) into many headings. Many writers would never think of using this typeface; indeed, it was a rare choice even for me, since it takes so much time to read. But Sara is a person who takes time. She is a patient and intuitive psychotherapist with a strong Eastern cultural influence. She works at a measured pace and gives her clients lots of room to explore and grow. A bold Helvetica typeface would have created a completely different and inaccurate impression.

Margaret's résumé, on the following page, conveys a different impression, yet one well-suited to her personality. Margaret is a direct person with simple interests whose sense of identity focuses primarily on her career. Incidentally, this is also a mature person who wished to deemphasize her age, and we did so by listing the dates she worked in smaller type, positioned at the end of each line instead of at the front. Notice also how a string of temporary positions are pulled together to convey a sense of cohesiveness for that first time period noted.

As noted, résumés deserve to be printed on résumé-quality paper; that means at least a twenty-four-pound weight. Choose an off-white color that can stand out from all the stark white papers lying on most desks, pale enough so that you can print and copy your résumé without losing clarity. Look also for interesting textures and speckled papers. Interesting paper is a relatively easy choice that adds style.

Margaret E. Resume

114 Summer Street
Fictiontown, Massachusetts 55555
(555) 555-5555

SUMMARY OF QUALIFICATIONS

Energetic and capable business professional with diverse skills.
Smart, personable and accountable for own work.
Rarely absent, with high level of company loyalty.
Relates easily with people, honestly and directly.
Notary Public in seventh term.
Types 50 wpm; some word processing experience.
Prefers part-time position, no weekends.

EMPLOYMENT

Bookkeeper, Office Manager and **Salesperson**, 1990 - present
Various locations in Central Massachusetts
Assumed a variety of responsibilities in temporary, part-time and freelance capacity. Maintained books, handled payroll and performed routine office functions. Prepared quotes for an electrician. Handled books for a local restaurant. Sold products for a plastic resins company.

Purchasing Agent, 1955 - 1990
Papa's Plastics, Inc., Greenfield, Massachusetts
Advanced in the company from the position of Assistant Purchasing Agent and Receptionist. Purchased all materials pertaining to production. Approved invoices and purchase orders. Ensured timely delivery of materials. Monitored activities in the warehouse and maintained contact with employees in order to respond to their special needs or requests. Prepared financial reports. Handled all company airline and hotel reservations. Assumed accounts payable duties as needed (posted billings, wrote checks, reconciled journals). Operated switchboard.

EDUCATION

Basic Income Tax Preparation (6 mos + internship), H&R Block
Traffic Management and Freight Rate (2 semesters), City Junior College
High School graduate

REFERENCES furnished upon request.

Figure 11. Margaret *after*

The psychology of color tells us that hue exerts an influence on readers; navy blue, for example, reminds us of uniforms and inspires respect. Rose is a warm, feminine color. Greens and browns are reminiscent of nature and natural settings. I could go on; however, I have found that when people simply select what most attracts them, those colors and textures will naturally fit and reflect their own personal style. Keep these things in mind when dressing for an interview too.

"But I have no skills!" I am often surprised at the people who tell me this. You might guess that it is one of my pet peeves. There is no such thing as a person with no skills! I like to illustrate this reality by describing a young man I will call Frankie. When I knew him, I was doing some work at a program for disadvantaged youth in Massachusetts. At the time, Massachusetts had the highest unemployment rate in the country, and the town of Fitchburg had the highest unemployment rate in the state. Frankie lived in the poorest part of town, where drug dealing appeared to be the predominant profession. None of Frankie's friends had ever had jobs, and most of their single parents had never worked either. But with a little effort and a good résumé, Frankie landed a job. A modified version of the résumé we prepared for that effort appears below. Frankie is proof that no one is hopeless; indeed, his future looked bright.

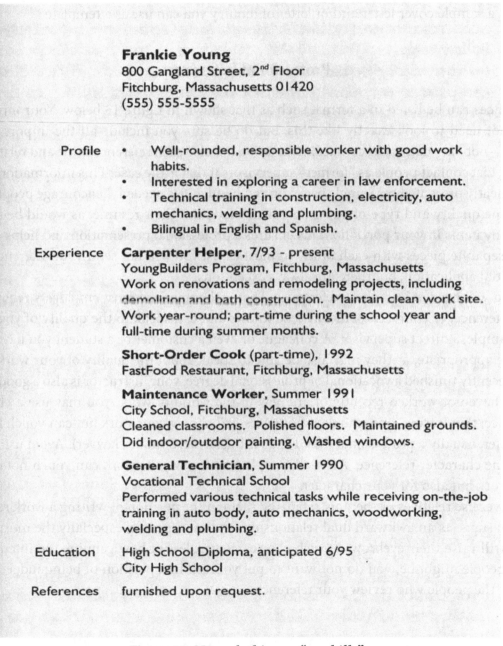

Frankie Young
800 Gangland Street, 2nd Floor
Fitchburg, Massachusetts 01420
(555) 555-5555

Profile	• Well-rounded, responsible worker with good work habits.
	• Interested in exploring a career in law enforcement.
	• Technical training in construction, electricity, auto mechanics, welding and plumbing.
	• Bilingual in English and Spanish.

Experience **Carpenter Helper**, 7/93 - present
YoungBuilders Program, Fitchburg, Massachusetts
Work on renovations and remodeling projects, including demolition and bath construction. Maintain clean work site. Work year-round; part-time during the school year and full-time during summer months.

Short-Order Cook (part-time), 1992
FastFood Restaurant, Fitchburg, Massachusetts

Maintenance Worker, Summer 1991
City School, Fitchburg, Massachusetts
Cleaned classrooms. Polished floors. Maintained grounds. Did indoor/outdoor painting. Washed windows.

General Technician, Summer 1990
Vocational Technical School
Performed various technical tasks while receiving on-the-job training in auto body, auto mechanics, woodworking, welding and plumbing.

Education High School Diploma, anticipated 6/95
City High School

References furnished upon request.

Figure 12. No such thing as "no skills"

Earlier I spoke about the professional portfolio and the various pieces of it. To optimize career success, once you put together a strong résumé, you will need to gather a portfolio of accompaniments that may include some or all of the following:

- a neatly typed list of references
- three or more letters of recommendation
- work samples and/or writing samples
- transcripts, certificates, licenses, or test scores
- lists of workshops or training seminars completed
- other addenda detailing pertinent achievements
- a sample cover letter and/or letter of inquiry you can use as a template

Professional References

References can be listed in a format such as that shown in figure 13 below. Your formatting does not need to look exactly like this, but do be sure you include all the important data points—not only name and contact information but also each reference's title and relationship to you. List contact people as "former" supervisors if that is the case. This information should all be neatly presented on a single page you can hand out as needed. I encourage people to use the same quality and type of paper on which they print their résumé, as would be the case for many items in your portfolio. This ensures a professional presentation and helps connect those separate pieces with each other. In most cases, you will not send your references with the initial application, but there are always exceptions.

You will need at least three references. That is the standard most employers require. The best reference, of course, is someone who knows and can speak to the quality of your work, for example, a direct supervisor. A colleague or even a customer or a student you have taught may be appropriate, as they may also be able to speak about the quality of your work. If you have recently finished a vocational or professional degree, your instructor is also a good choice. If you have not worked recently or are new to the world of work, you may use a character reference; that is, someone who does not necessarily know your work but can vouch for your character, usually a professional friend (e.g., minister, accountant, lawyer). Avoid using more than one character reference. After all, people who know your work can vouch not only for your work but also for your character.

Never use relatives or therapists; putting them in the position of writing a work reference for you suggests an awkward dual relationship, and most people, especially the most ethical ones, will raise their eyebrows at such choices. Regardless of how genuine the intentions of these people might be, you do not want to put yourself in a position of being judged in this way by the people who review your references.

References for David Fender

101 Reggae Street ♥ New York, New York, 10001
(555) 555-5555 ♥ davidfender@yahoo.com

♥ Eileen Towards Jazz
Manager
Data R Us, Harvard Satellite Office
Street Address
City, New Hampshire 00001

Supervisor
(617) 555-5555
notarealemail@gmail.com

♥ Gimmy A. Break
Senior Account Executive
Fox Industries
Street Address
Portland, Maine 00001

Former Colleague
(612) 555-0000
alsonotarealemail@yahoo.com

♥ Ahmed Ali, PhD
Professor of Music
State University
Street Address
Boston, Massachusetts 00001

Former Professor
(216) 555-0000
alsonotarealemail@fmail.com

Figure 13. Sample list of references

People who have had multiple careers may have different references they will want to use for different positions. Being selective about who can provide the best reference for each position to which you apply is a good idea, and the reference list is easy enough to tailor. Get into the habit of asking the people with whom you've had good working relationships, particularly in the moment of departing from that professional relationship, if they would be willing to provide a reference for you in the future—or even write a letter for you. Then jot down all their contact information before you forget. Keep a running list and call upon the references you need when you need them.

Another vehicle for gathering references today is through social networking. Do not be afraid to ask that same reference who thinks so highly of you to share his or her thoughts in a paragraph or two on LinkedIn.com, for example. You can return the favor by writing up an endorsement for them. (You can create your professional network at www.linkedin.com.)

Letters of Recommendation

It is important to understand the difference between a reference and letter of recommendation. A reference is simply a person willing and able to provide information about a potential applicant, usually over the phone but increasingly in an online form or email. A letter of recommendation, on the other hand, is an actual letter on professional letterhead in which a selected reference details in writing his or her relationship and experience with the person for whom he or she is providing the reference.

I encourage people to submit a reference packet when references are requested; include the list of references as a cover page, with selected letters of recommendation attached. The letters do not need to correspond precisely with the contacts listed on the reference sheet. In fact, there are times when it may be difficult to trust just what a reference might say about you over the phone, and you may prefer to simply submit a letter you have been able to review and not list that person as a reference. Use common sense, and trust your intuition when making these decisions.

Letters of recommendation are valuable for a variety of reasons:

- They can detail your strengths precisely. If they do not, you can speak with the writer to suggest changes; for example, remind them of a particularly important achievement they may have forgotten to mention. Most people (especially the ones who really like you) will be more than happy to take your feedback.
- You know exactly what the letters say. No surprises.
- Letters of recommendation may save an interviewer time. I remember an instance where a person I counseled went to her interview with her packet ready and handed it to the interviewer, who replied, "These are excellent letters. I'm going to go ahead and offer you the job; I don't have the time to call on all those references for the other applicants."
- Letters of recommendation can record work you did for someone who may no longer be available by phone or at all. Things happen, sometimes suddenly and unexpectedly. Suppose the person who knows you best suddenly moves out of the country, or worse, develops early-onset Alzheimer's and can no longer remember you and the great relationship you had. Err on the safe side. Get their words on paper while you can and while it is still fresh in their minds.

As noted, letters of recommendation must always be signed and presented on the author's letterhead, not yours. A good copy of the original letter is fine to pass on to a prospective employer. (Save the original, in case someone ever wants to see it, and use that version to copy from.)

Finally, do not be afraid to help someone write your letter of recommendation. Busy professionals often have others assist in writing letters and documents that they are still willing to sign, so long as the contents accurately reflect their views. You know better than anyone else all the wonderful work you have done in the past, and you can remind the former employer of those things—even suggest wording. Many letters of recommendation fail to get written because the task keeps falling to the bottom of the inbox. It does take some effort; if you can ease the process at all, be willing to make the offer.

A sample letter of recommendation appears on the following page. Note that it appears on formal letterhead and that it tends to follow a predictable flow that includes

- the date on which the letter was written;
- a greeting ("To whom it may concern" is fine; this after all is a letter that will be used for a variety of recipients);
- a statement that explains the relationship of the writer to the subject of the reference, ideally including how long the two have been acquainted;
- a description of the person's strengths and specific support of the statements made (vague references to a person's "greatness" are not helpful; the best letters give specific examples); and
- a closing paragraph that includes the statement of recommendation ("recommend without reservation," "strongly recommend," or just "recommend" are all appropriate); some will also invite further conversation and leave contact information; that is entirely optional.

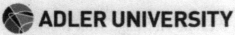

ADLER UNIVERSITY

17 North Dearborn Street | tel 312.662.4000
Chicago, Illinois 60602 | fax 312.662.4099

May 6, 2016

To whom it may concern:

Please accept this letter of recommendation for **Susan Strong**, a promising young clinician I had the pleasure to meet in April 2015. I met Ms. Strong through a professional friend and colleague, and although I have never directly supervised her work, I have had an opportunity to become acquainted with her through an informal mentoring relationship, including a lively professional correspondence as she has pursued her social work degree and license.

Ms. Strong has experienced considerable success in her academic pursuits and seems to have an insatiable appetite for learning. I'm impressed with her commitment to continuing education; she seems to add new tools to her toolbox at every opportunity, all aimed at helping her to become an ever more skilled and effective practitioner. She frequently reaches out to ask my opinion on various matters concerning her professional development.

I have found Ms. Strong to be inquisitive, self-directed, courageous, respectful and resolute. She is a "high achiever" in every respect, open to feedback and smart in her discernment of how to apply her learning to practice and to her own self-improvement. She would be a delight to supervise, and I am confident that she will indeed be an asset wherever she decides to plant her flag. It would be the good fortune of any prospective employer to add her to their ranks.

It is without reservation that I recommend Susan Strong for employment and for any further educational pursuits that ignite her interest.

Sincerely,

Haley Fox, PhD

Haley Fox, PhD
Core Faculty, Counseling and Art Therapy

hf

adler.edu

Figure 14. Sample letter of recommendation

Cover Letters

The best cover letter is tailored to a particular job or lead, and the more information you have before writing it, the better. Try to get the name and title of the person in charge of hiring and as much information about the job itself as possible. It is worth a phone call or two or at the very least a careful perusal of the company website to gather that information.

A sample cover letter appears on the following page. Similar to the letter of recommendation already shared, the letter is signed and printed on letterhead. I have used David Fender as an example again, so you can see how his letterhead uses the same font, style, and paper as his résumé. This sends the message that it is the same person and helps to ensure that pages, if they become separated, can easily be recognized and brought back together. You will also notice that the body of every cover letter is similar to a letter of recommendation, in that it has three basic parts.

David Fender

101 Reggae Street ♥ New York, New York, 10001
(555) 555-5555 ♥ davidfender@yahoo.com

October 10, 2000

John Employer
ABC Technology
123 Alphabet Park
Hancock, Virginia 66666

Dear Mr. Employer:

Please accept my enclosed résumé in application for the position **Account Executive**, which I saw advertised in Sunday's *Gazette*.

Over the past decade, I have enjoyed substantial success as a salesperson, primarily in the restaurant and music industries. Beginning with leads provided by my employer and eventually progressing to cold calls with contacts I found through my own research, I increased the accounts at my most recent place of employment by 35% over the course of one year. Selling is a passion of mine; I enjoy my contacts, and I always strive to present myself in a straight-forward and professional way. My supervisor describes my sales skills as "superb." More details about my experience can be found in my résumé, attached.

I will be calling you on Thursday to ensure you have received my application materials and to see when we might be able to get together to talk more about your needs and my qualifications. In the meantime, have a great day!

Sincerely,

David Fender

Enclosure: Resume

Figure 15. Sample cover letter

In the first paragraph of the body of the cover letter, state your intent; that is, answer the question, "Why am I writing this letter?" The second and/or third paragraphs allow you to call attention to your résumé, to highlight what you want noticed, and to add any details about your qualifications that may not be included or fully detailed in the résumé. Here you answer the question, "Why should you hire me?" And in the final paragraph, be sure to indicate the "next step." The more proactive, the better. I encourage people to take the lead in follow-up and to show your reader your willingness to do so. Too many times I hear from job applicants bemoaning the painful "waiting to hear back" from an employer. There is no reason why you cannot politely offer to take the bull by the horns and schedule a follow-up contact yourself. When you do call, the employer might say something like, "It will be at least three weeks before we schedule interviews," to which you can respond, "Okay, I will plan on waiting three weeks until I try to contact you again." Then put it in your calendar and show the employer that you are a person who keeps commitments. Call back on the day you say you will.

Once you have your résumé and portfolio in order, you may find it to be useful in several ways. First of all, the process of writing a résumé will have made you more aware of your gifts and talents and will likely have boosted your confidence about landing a job—the right job. You can then use your résumé as a vehicle for applying for advertised openings or for making inquiries with people who may not be advertising but with whom you are interested in working. Such inquiries may put you in a position to learn about unadvertised openings and also to begin to develop professional relationships through informational interviewing. I have included a sample letter of inquiry below to illustrate how you might approach such an instance.

Also, keep in mind that similar materials and approaches are required for unpaid experiences like internships. Check out step 6 for more on this topic.

Before you get too far into your job search, make sure you have a plan. A plan can further narrow your focus and guide you in setting monthly goals and daily tasks to guide you as you set about giving more substance to the images you have called forth.

CARMEN CURIOUS

February 20, 2017

Rich Richman
Human Resources Manager
Rich Technologies
420 Wealth Parkway
Springfield, CC 00000

Dear Mr. Richman:

I hope this letter finds you well. I send warm regards from Susan Friendly, who suggested I contact you to inquire about opportunities at Rich Technologies.

I made Susan's acquaintance in graduate school, where we are both studying to be human resource professionals. She learned that I was thinking of moving to Springfield after graduation and encouraged me to send you my resume, enclosed. Susan has decided to remain in Collegeville and is lining up job interviews here.

As you can see from my resume, I have previous experience as an administrative secretary in a company similar to Rich Technologies. There I developed a fondness for the industry and gained a reputation for being able to "speak the language" of engineers and to get their questions answered quickly and efficiently. As a new professional in human resources, I have a special interest in health benefits and employee assistance, and I am eager to apply and grow my skills in a setting like yours.

I would love to talk more about your needs and my qualifications. Feel free to contact me at the email address listed below or on my personal cell phone (xxx-xxx-xxxx) if you have any questions or would just like to set up a time. As I am planning a visit to Springfield soon, I will plan on calling you next Thursday to ensure that you've received my letter and to see if we can work anything out for next month.

Thank you for your time and interest!

Carmen Curious

Street Address, City, ST ZIP Code Country
phone number | fax number
e-mail address | Web site

Figure 16. Letter of inquiry

Preparing for Change: Goal-Setting and Planning

In the first edition of this book, I spent a fair amount of time walking the reader through a process of setting and working toward actionable career goals. I had my own preferred way of doing and teaching this, beginning with a values assessment and then prioritizing daily tasks that supported those values and larger goals. I developed my own tools and forms to support those efforts. My approach did not differ greatly from approaches promoted by other therapists and life coaches.

Recently, however, I had a bit of an epiphany. Around the first of the year, I looked at a long list of goals that had sat on my list of things to do for a long time, not moving, and I decided to change my approach. The stress of regularly looking at that list and feeling guilty about not completing it finally got to be too much for me. So, I set the list aside and simply adopted a daily routine I felt I could stick with. The items I put on the list (like the goals I had set for myself) were congruent with the things most important to me. They were also manageable. I could complete the entire list in an hour. But I didn't micromanage myself with it. I simply wrote the list of daily items on a small whiteboard that I stuck on my refrigerator, and I made this rule for myself: no television or supper until that list was complete. Here is a copy of my list.

- ☐ write in gratitude journal
- ☐ meditate for fifteen minutes
- ☐ do five-minute yoga stretches
- ☐ do ten squats
- ☐ floss
- ☐ sing at least one song
- ☐ write something original

The first five items kept me healthy and destressed, and I knew them to be far better coping strategies than eating or watching television; this is the recognition that first led me to my rule (no television or supper until the list is complete). The last two items fed my deepest career-related passions as a singer/songwriter and as a writer. It is important to note that I was very easy on myself. I can crank out a song in about three minutes, and when I said, "write something original," I let myself check that item off if I only wrote one original sentence. The wisdom underlying this approach escaped me at first, but in retrospect, it occurs to me that I can probably expect to spend more time on those last two items once I get started—because I love them! The hardest part for me was always starting, so I had to make this daily routine doable.

Primary among that long list of unfinished projects were several writing projects. I had many books, articles, and blogs in me, and I had been keeping a list of them for years. My life was busy, however, and I kept waiting for a week or even a long weekend that would allow me time to make real headway. That long weekend never came. Consequently, I robbed myself of the joy of writing—and I robbed the world of some fresh, new creative works.

As I sat at my computer (about suppertime) on January 1 and tried to think of something original to write, I drew a blank for about a minute. Then I pulled that list out of my drawer and selected one of the writing projects there, an article on art-based research I had been putting off, a summary of my 2005 dissertation research—and I started cranking it out. Every day I wrote a little bit more, sometimes only a paragraph, but on the weekend, I was on fire. I finished the entire article in about two weeks. Then I pulled my list out again, and I decided it was time for a new edition of *Follow Your Bliss*. And here I am, nearly complete—and it has only been two weeks.

Mind you, I am as busy as I ever was, now a professor of counseling and art therapy at Adler University. I am also taking on a time-limited project to help design a doctoral program by March of this year, tending to relationships with my four young adult children, and finding time for my significant other. Life continues to interrupt, as it always has.

Around the same time I began this new daily routine approach, I read an article by James Clear (2017). I recommend that you read it too. Mr. Clear appears to have made a similar discovery, which he conceptualizes as an essential difference between goals and systems. He asked the question, "If you completely ignored your goals and focused only on your system, would you still get results?" I am here to tell you, for me personally, I got even quicker results, even better, just a few weeks after changing my approach. I also reduced my television viewing and was more mindful of my eating habits, and I could not be more pleased about that result.

Now, this is not to say that goals are bad. Indeed, had I not written that list of goals, I would have been at a bit of a loss when it came to completing my daily task of writing something original. So, I will include the material I shared in the first edition, with some minor editing. I am hopeful that you too will end up with a list of honorable and enriching goals that fit well into your values and will contribute to your own pursuit of bliss. Keep them handy when you need inspiration in your daily routine.

I recall the eagerness with which my bouncing niece looked forward to her entry into the first grade. For weeks, her grandmother, "Nona," had been telling her of the many adventures that awaited her at "the big school." Elaine looked forward with the greatest anticipation to learning to read. Oh, how she wanted to read all by herself! Her excitement piqued as she set off on that first day of school. But when Nona greeted her at the end of the day, it was a devastated little girl who stepped off the school bus to meet her. "Nona!" she exclaimed, despairing and incredulous. "I can't read!"

Lainey did not learn to read overnight, but she did learn to read. Change usually does not happen overnight. More often, it requires a conscious commitment followed by careful and mindful planning.

Change begins with the courage to imagine a goal, and it is significantly empowered by the mere writing down of that goal. I always caution people: be careful what you wish for; it might come true! In my own life, I am accustomed to writing (and periodically reviewing) a five-year plan, and once I write down my intentions, they seem to take on a life of their own. In my midtwenties, I wrote that I would like to have three children over the course of five years. I had three children in three years—and a "bonus" before the fifth year came! I also decided that I would very much like to teach in a university. I actually broke that goal down into doable chunks, to include pursuit of a doctoral degree in addition to several other steps along the way. Almost in spite of my plan, I found myself on a university faculty within a year of writing that goal—without having yet acquired or even begun working on a doctorate. I have an acquaintance who tells me he has never failed to achieve a goal he has written down. What power! It seems prudent, before writing them down, to be a bit discerning about what goal or goals to choose.

Priorities

Most planning systems begin with goal-setting. I suggest beginning first with carefully assessing your priorities—and by that, in keeping with the overall theme of this book, I mean not so much what you want or desire but rather what the universe needs or desires from you. This task should follow completion of the self-awareness exercises already presented, so that you may begin with a good sense of your values and dominant qualities—and bliss.

Start with exercise 12 on the following page. Look at the different groupings that can be used to organize your priorities, including the one in diagram form below. Think of a grouping or list of three to seven priority areas that resonate with you. You might first sketch or draw a list on some scratch paper. When you have settled on a list that works for you, enter it into the table following the examples provided.

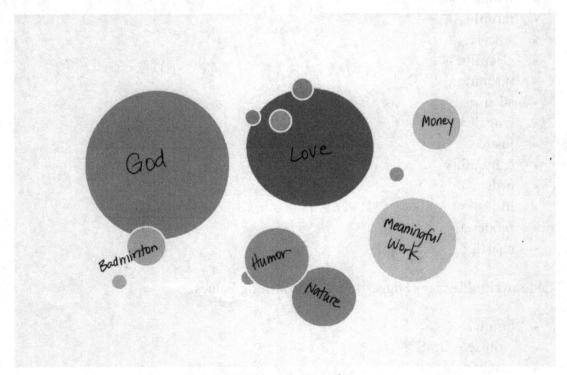

Figure 17. Priorities in a diagram

Exercise 12: Prioritizing

Make a list of what is most important to you, say, three to seven priority areas. They can be characterized any way that is meaningful to you; a few examples follow.

Body	Material possessions	Money
Mind	Personal growth and healing	Golf
Spirit	Professional development	Sex and intimacy
	Financial security	Status/power

Learning new things
Making a difference
Being outdoors
Loving others
Self-expression

Creativity
Personal health and well-being
Marriage, children, and family
Home and environment
Spirituality and the planet

Benjamin Franklin's Thirteen Virtues

- temperance
- humility
- sincerity
- cleanliness
- resolution
- silence
- frugality
- justice
- tranquility
- order
- industry
- moderation
- chastity

The Franklin Planner's Suggestions for Governing Values

- family
- culture/education
- career
- spirituality

Rank Order	List of Priorities
[ ]	
[ ]	
[ ]	
[ ]	
[ ]	
[ ]	
[ ]	

Goal-Setting

With your priorities clearly stated in the table above, now set aside that paperwork and start fresh with goal-setting. That's right. Disregard the list you have just completed. Do not force its influence upon your goal-setting. Goal-setting works best, I believe, as a parallel process. That is, instead of setting goals based on your stated priorities, simply try to write down some goals, any goals about which you might feel passionate. Then use your list of priorities later to check how the goals fit with them.

Let me explain with an example. It might be the case that physical well-being is number one in importance for you, but this should not dictate that you then set a primary goal related to supporting your physical health. On the contrary, you may already be acting as an excellent steward of the health of your body and feel no need to change your established sleep, eating, and exercise routine. You may, in fact, choose to work exclusively on career goals in the coming year. There is nothing wrong with that.

The point here is actually heightened self-awareness. If you have chosen goals that fit into certain priority areas, can you live with that? Or will that new information lead you to go back to the drawing board, so to speak, to modify your goals based on what you know about your priorities?

Before starting the process of writing down goals, I recommend taking ten to fifteen minutes to do some mindfulness meditation to get yourself relaxed and centered.

Exercise 13: Goal-Setting

After getting yourself relaxed and centered, spend a few moments brainstorming some three-to-five-year goals—achievements or milestones uniquely suited to you, particularly those that could meaningfully contribute to the world or put you in better stead to do so. Jot down whatever comes to mind on paper in whatever form they emerge (words, images, diagrams, phrases), using the space provided on the following page.

To really free your imagination, I encourage you not only to jot down your ideas but take the time to create a vision board. Find a large poster board or foam-core board. Grab some magazines and pull out images and words you are drawn to; look for items that jump out at you from the page. Gather them and fashion them into a collage.

When the piece seems complete, spend some time reflecting upon it, and see if you can translate what you see into "goal" language. For example, if you find a scene from a part of the world to which you feel drawn, perhaps a goal might involve traveling there for work or pleasure.

Use the space below to sketch out your vision board ideas.

Once you have discerned three to five goals from your vision board, enter them into the first column of the table below. Compare the goals with the priorities you've already written, and note any priorities that are supported by the goals you have listed.

Long-Term Goals	Relevant Priorities

As you choose your goals, remember the power they hold. When you dare to articulate goals, your heart, your mind, and your awareness open to possibilities that might otherwise have eluded you. You may recognize opportunities that cross your path, and you are likely to take advantage of at least some of them. I recall listening to someone lecture about "visionary thinking" many years ago. The speaker shared her desire to own a little red sports car. At first, she hesitated to even entertain the thought, as the possibility seemed remote to her. But one day, she gave herself permission to envision herself in that little red sports car in great detail. She immediately began to see little red sports cars everywhere she went. Within three weeks, she was driving one. The image had been so clear in her mind that when she glimpsed the very car she desired out of the corner of her eye while passing a dealer's lot, it virtually jumped out at her.

This stage of envisioning goals can be rich and exciting. Sadly, self-sabotage can also rear its naughty head at this early stage. (I will discuss self-sabotage in some detail in step 6.) So be mindful of the goals you set for yourself. Be sure they are your own goals and not things you have been told you "should" do or be—and make sure you allow yourself to dream.

Exercise 13: Goal-Setting (continued)

Now take each long-term goal and set at least two to three short-term goals (a few months to several months in duration) that will contribute to each goal's successful completion. Write these into one of the tables on the pages that follow.

After writing in each short-term goal, come up with some reasonable and doable daily tasks. For each task, rank the order of priority (with "A" being high, "B" being moderate, and "C" being low), and estimate a projected completion date. Enter those into the table as well.

You will need several copies of this half-page form in order to fully address each short-term goal. Use one half-page form for each short-term goal.

The next step will be to enter daily tasks into the proper dates in your personal calendar or daily planner. Then all you need is to complete the tasks to which you have committed yourself.

Long-Range Goal		Relevant Priority or Priorities
Short-Term Goal 1		
A, B, C (Rank)	Daily Tasks	Projected Completion

Long-Range Goal		Relevant Priority or Priorities
Short-Term Goal 2		
A, B, C (Rank)	Daily Tasks	Projected Completion

Long-Range Goal		Relevant Priority or Priorities
Short-Term Goal 3		
A, B, C (Rank)	Daily Tasks	Projected Completion

Long-Range Goal		Relevant Priority or Priorities
Short-Term Goal 4		

A, B, C (Rank)	Daily Tasks	Projected Completion

Long-Range Goal		Relevant Priority or Priorities
Short-Term Goal 5		

A, B, C (Rank)	Daily Tasks	Projected Completion

Long-Range Goal	Relevant Priority or Priorities

Short-Term Goal 6		
A, B, C (Rank)	Daily Tasks	Projected Completion

Long-Range Goal	Relevant Priority or Priorities

Short-Term Goal 7		
A, B, C (Rank)	Daily Tasks	Projected Completion

Long-Range Goal	Relevant Priority or Priorities

Short-Term Goal 8	

A, B, C (Rank)	Daily Tasks	Projected Completion

Long-Range Goal	Relevant Priority or Priorities

Short-Term Goal 9	

A, B, C (Rank)	Daily Tasks	Projected Completion

A, B, C (Rank)	Daily Tasks	Projected Completion

Long-Range Goal | Relevant Priority or Priorities

Short-Term Goal 10

Let's walk through an example. First, let's suppose a fictional fellow named Pat came up with a list of priorities from the above example and ranked them as follows.

Rank Order	List of Priorities
[3]	Body
[2]	Mind
[1]	Spirit
[ ]	
[ ]	
[ ]	
[ ]	

Figure 18. Prioritizing example

Next, Pat sets aside his priorities and comes up with four goals that come to mind. He feels some passion behind each of the goals.

Long-Term Goals	Relevant Priorities
Lose 25 lbs.	
Put in a patio garden.	
Improve relations w/my son.	
Learn to use a spreadsheet.	

Figure 19. Goal-setting example a

Then, Pat examines his goals and decides which priorities fit them.

Long-Term Goals	Relevant Priorities
Lose 25 lbs.	Body (3)
Put in a patio garden.	Body (3) and spirit (1)
Improve relations w/my son.	Spirit (1)
Learn to use a spreadsheet.	Mind (2)

Figure 20. Goal-setting example b

Pat has chosen goals that fit well with his priorities. He sees that two goals address his spiritual well-being, a pleasant surprise. Based on his observations, he decides to keep and to work with all these goals. Now he must expand upon each. A page concerning his goal to improve his relationship with his son appears below.

Pat will need to complete several of these sheets and then enter pertinent tasks into his calendar or planner. In most cases, each long-range goal he sets will require more than one short-term goal and many smaller tasks. Breaking the process down increases one's appreciation for just what is required to achieve something. Sometimes it may cause us to rethink our goals before moving ahead with them; this pause can help us to see what lies ahead and to reaffirm our commitment to proceed.

Long-Range Goal		Relevant Priority or Priorities
Improve relations w/my son.		*Spirit and Body*

	Short-Term Goal #2	
	Make the commitment to shoot hoops together once a week.	

A, B, C (Rank)	Daily Tasks	Projected Completion
A	*Agree on a day/time that works for us.*	*Tonight! 9pm, 4/8*
A	*Clear my schedule; put it in my calendar.*	*4/9*
A	*Be open to conversation; ask about his life.*	*ongoing*

Figure 21. Goal-planning example

Notice that the short-term goal Pat chose here actually meets two of his stated priorities: both spirit and body. He may not have anticipated this, as it would not have necessarily occurred to him that the goal to improve his relationship with his son might also contribute to a healthier body. Such happy occurrences naturally flow from trusting bliss to show you the way.

Keep in mind as well that those daily and weekly routines may be even more responsible for helping you achieve a more bliss-filled life than the long-term goals you have set. Remember James Clear's eye-opening experience discussed earlier.

Time/Event Management

The term *time management,* while widely used, is a bit of a misnomer. Time is a finite quantity. It is not a commodity we can "save" or expand. We have what we have. What we can manage are the events we engage in the finite time we have available.

One of the most important lessons about time that I ever learned was the difference between urgent and important, an idea advanced by Stephen Covey (1989). An urgent task is one that calls for an immediate response: the phone rings, someone knocks at the door, you sever your arm in a horrible accident. Whether or not the event is important to you personally, it demands a response.

Important tasks, on the other hand, may or may not be urgent, but they are tasks you have assigned a high value. Most people know these most important tasks in their hearts—or in some cases finally realize them near the end of lives. When these important things knock loudly at your door, they generally do so only when they have been ignored repeatedly; even then, some people still will not let themselves be distracted by them, preoccupied as we tend to be with urgent matters. It is up to you to prioritize these important matters, to make time to attend to them, and such a priority may require a deliberate effort.

Covey eloquently describes the relationship between important and urgent tasks in his "time management matrix" (1989, 151), which I have simplified below. Any task, Covey explains, can be described in terms of its importance and its urgency. Those tasks that are most critical to attend to in service of achieving new goals fall into the "important" and "not urgent" category (cell 2). You can treat them as more urgent by incorporating time-limited tasks to support them in your daily or weekly routine. The outcomes of taking this deliberate step are well worth the effort.

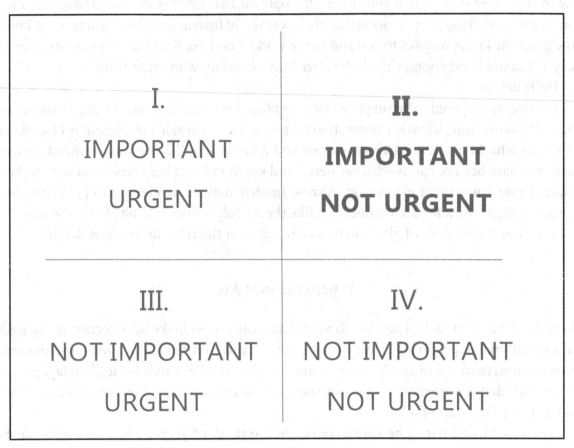

Figure 22. Covey's time management matrix

This has been a somewhat abbreviated look at goals and planning, but there is already a multitude of resources available. The value-based Franklin Covey Day Planner system has held a fine reputation for a long time, but it has become a bit pricey, in my view. You can look over your options at http://www.franklincovey.com. Other viable options exist too. Artsy types may especially enjoy the new product of a recent KickStarter effort, *Rituals for Living Dreambook,* available at http://dreambook.vision/. Find an option that fits you. My own go-to is my computer-based, color-coded Outlook calendar.

Many other things can be said about time management, but the final message I feel compelled to leave you with is this: the most important thing you can do to keep yourself on the right track is to unceasingly follow your bliss. This means remaining mindful of and true to your stated goals, of course, but it also means not subjecting yourself to needless suffering. If you are suffering, you may want to reflect upon whether you may have set the wrong goals for yourself. Most importantly, it means maintaining an acute awareness of the bliss that calls you every day in small ways. It is never too soon to begin listening to your heart when you feel pulled in a particular direction. Do not wait until you have fully figured out all the details for pursuing some major overarching goal you might have fantasized about. If you are meant to reach that goal, then trust that the little moments of bliss along the way will guide you there.

Go ahead and phone that person who has been on your mind. Sign up for that class you saw in the paper that piqued your interest. Apply for that job you saw advertised that made you tingle. Too many people rationalize their way out of listening to their hearts. Who knows how great the losses may be, to you and to the world. You have heard the arguments, "I'm too busy"; "I'm not good enough"; "Maybe after I get caught up with other things."

Do it now.

Finally, be prepared to be surprised by your bliss. Seemingly unrelated things may beckon you at the same time; let your imagination take hold. I am reminded of a seminar I facilitated, a woman who had a new paralegal degree and a love for birds. She was stumped. But she dared to share both passions with her peers, and she found that her combination of interests inspired everyone else's imagination. Almost immediately, someone piped up, "What about doing paralegal work for an organization like the Audubon Society?" She loved the idea.

Trusting the wisdom of bliss can be a challenge, but the rewards are considerable.

Where the Jobs Are

Newspaper-based classified ads (available electronically now) make up a portion of job leads, but a much smaller portion than most people realize, and it is growing smaller. Most jobs come from unadvertised openings. It is important to approach the search for leads imaginatively. I have included a worksheet to get you started. It begins on the following page, and I will elaborate on each part of it.

Before reading further, be sure to remember to think of yourself as your most valuable resource. Have you made a commitment to devote your time and talent to your job search? What about your family, the significant people in your life, especially the people with whom you live? Are they supportive of your career goals? Talk with them about what the job search will mean to the family in terms of time and tasks, and discuss what you will need from each other.

Once you have made a commitment to be your own champion in this endeavor, make a list of everyone you know.

This may be an overstatement; but do not underutilize this area! The people who know you best will be your best advocates and will go that extra mile to inform you and promote you to people they know. The categories listed in exercise 15 are intended to stimulate your imagination and memory. An interesting twist on the simple laundry list is something called a *social atom*. The social atom is a bit like a genogram, except that it does not require standard symbols to represent relationships; rather, you get full creative freedom to create a diagram of all the significant people in your life. A diagram of this sort lets you not only consider your contacts but also the weight of their importance to you and the ways in which each of them is connected to you and to each other.

After you have brainstormed, select those contacts you wish to include in your job-seeking network and enter their names in the table on the next page. Think of the array of ways in which people might be helpful to you, not only as direct sources of job leads but also for their encouragement, support, and imagination. Choose people who like you and care about you and people you would genuinely like to know better.

Exercise 14: Social Atom

In the space below, or better yet on a separate larger piece of paper, create a diagram that illustrates all the people in your life and the quality of those relationships. First represent yourself (with a simple shape or symbol), then add every significant relationship you can think of. Consider the distances you put between yourself and others, and keep in mind that difficult relationships may actually rest quite close to you. Be creative in how you represent the various relationships in your social atom.

Use the space below to sketch out your social atom.

Exercise 15: Contact Lists

Use the following tables to brainstorm contacts, circling the most important ones, and then checking them off as you contact them and cultivate their help with your job search.

People Contacts
Friends (e.g., school/college friends, neighbors, children's friends, work friends)
Relatives
Community Contacts (e.g., merchants, hairdresser, mail carrier, bank teller)

Leisure-Time Acquaintances (e.g., clubs, fitness buddies, people from your place of worship, music/sports groups)

Job Contacts (e.g., current and former supervisors, colleagues, customers/clients)

Social Media Contacts and Groups (e.g., LinkedIn, Facebook, Twitter, Instagram)

Other Sources of Leads
Internet Search Engines
Pet Organizations and Professional Journals (print and online)
School-Based Resources (for alums)
State Unemployment Offices, Workforce Agencies, and Private Employment and Temp Agencies
Other (e.g., miscellaneous directories and other media)

Internet Search Engines

The fastest-growing job-hunting networks since the first edition of this book can be found on the Internet. Some of the more popular sites include Indeed, Monster.com, CareerBuilder, USAJobs, and even Craigslist. Robert Half (2018) identifies the top-ten Internet-based job search engines as follows:

1. Robert Half
2. CareerBuilder
3. Indeed
4. Job.com
5. Ladders
6. LinkedIn
7. Glassdoor
8. Monster
9. SimplyHired
10. USAJobs

If you are one of the rare people who still lacks access to or an awareness of how to navigate the Internet, your local librarian or state job service office may be able to acquaint you with the process of accessing information and sending and receiving electronic mail. Websites are growing and changing every day and are far too numerous to list here. Increasingly, employers only accept applications online. Find your favorite sites, and list them in the table above. Set up automatic alerts to receive notices pertinent to your interests.

When setting up those alerts, be mindful of the keywords you select. Too broad a term will result in overwhelming responses that take too long to peruse; too narrow a term will result in a paucity of leads. A skilled career counselor who knows you well can help you with this process.

I recommend first off that you remain aware of your nonnegotiables (e.g., those geographic locations beyond which you are not willing to go). Additionally, keep your bliss in mind; this will narrow your field in a way that prioritizes positions that will actually bring you joy. Open your mind to a variety of job titles that may be unfamiliar to you but may still encompass your skill set.

Emerging jobs that are not yet well known can pose particular challenges. Let us take an example. A new graduate in art therapy, full of excitement and anticipation, signs up on a job-search engine and plugs in the keywords "art + therapist." Starting this specifically is actually a good idea, I think, for any results will match the seeker's primary interest. However, I suspect the search will not reveal too many leads. That is not because there is no market for skilled art therapists; on the contrary, I have directly experienced the powerful efficacy of the work, and I know that once exposed to it, employers would value it, if only based on client outcomes. However, the job title "art therapist" is not one that appears often in print—for a variety of reasons. Some employers may not be familiar with the discipline; those who are may not have considered how well art therapy may work within their setting, and even those who understand and value art therapy may not have a classification available in their setting with that particular title. Many art therapists today are well-trained as primary clinicians (e.g., able to perform assessments; assign clinical diagnoses; deliver individual, group, and family therapy; and document their work through progress notes, reports, and discharge summaries). Many are license eligible as professional counselors or marriage and family therapists, in addition to having an art therapy credential. Thus, there is no reason why they could not fit nicely into a job title such as primary therapist, clinician, or mental-health practitioner, to name a few. The art therapy simply describes their way of working and perhaps their particular theoretical orientation. All this can be explained in an interview for any employer who has questions about the qualifications.

Pet Organizations and Professional Journals

What groups fit your identity and interests? Are you a neurodiverse person? A gamer? A birdwatcher? A Toastmaster? A *Star Trek* geek? A baseball fan? A theatergoer? A rare-coin collector? A professional counselor? A movie buff? A practicing Buddhist? An architect? A woman? These days, there is a group or organization for virtually every interest. I would recommend you be discerning and only join those groups for which you feel a strong connection and passion. (Follow your bliss.)

Many organizations may be able to help in a more general way, too. Chambers of commerce keep data on businesses and organizations and sometimes sponsor get-togethers that offer networking opportunities. Many social service organizations offer job-search assistance of various kinds. Look for private industry councils, regional employment boards, state-funded career centers, and also civic groups and religious organizations dedicated to assisting members with their career goals.

School-Based Resources

College and university and even high school guidance counselors and placement offices often offer free services and job leads to their alumni, as well as formal networking opportunities. Make an appointment to meet a particular person assigned to this role, if possible. This will extend your reach beyond what you can find perusing search engines on your own.

State and Private Employment Agencies

State employment agencies and each state's vocational rehabilitation agency are specifically designed to offer resources to support your job search. They offer classes, career counseling, and job listings, and they may be able to put your résumé on the Internet. Private employment agencies and headhunters are listed in the Yellow Pages and classified ads. Temporary agencies give you (and your employer) opportunities to test-drive a job while bringing home some income. Headhunting agencies are often specific to particular industries. Be sure you know the fees ahead of time.

Other Sources of Leads

For years, directories have been a valid source of job leads. Telephone books publish not only the Yellow Pages but also an array of business directories, including many targeted to specific businesses and industries. Have your local librarian point out directories specific to your industry and your geographical area. Nowadays, you can find an array of online phone directories, not only at many libraries but also on your own computer, cell phone, or other Internet-accessible device.

Radio and television stations, including cable stations, occasionally run listings as well as special informational programs for job seekers. (These often appear in the wee hours of the morning.)

Be creative, and do not forget word of mouth. Your personal network may be an excellent source of word-of-mouth recommendations, especially when it comes to people whose interests and skill sets most closely mirror your own. Keep conversations rolling within your personal and professional network, and keep your ear to the ground as you move through the world. You never know where and in what circumstance you may learn something relevant.

Be sure you remain alert (face out of your phone) to what is happening around you. Keep your eyes open for signs and new construction in areas where you would like to work. Bulletin boards are everywhere. Look for postings in churches, schools, laundromats, grocery stores, libraries, offices—the list is endless. Many companies post internally before advertising to the general public. You may be able to add more to this list. Grab extra paper and write down all your ideas.

Finally, get leads from your leads. Have others keep ears and eyes open for you. Every time you make a contact, you are just a question away from another contact. Most people are happy to share ideas with you; genuine enthusiasm is contagious. Do you not love it when you make somebody's day just by sharing some information?

Classified Ads and Job Postings

Whether you locate these in print or electronic media, every job search will eventually lead to a brief and specific written statement about the job description and requirements. Use these postings creatively. Do not limit yourself to one source. Use the major job search engines, but also check out local media and special interest groups. Read the business section to keep abreast of what is happening in your community, particularly new business openings and companies that appear to be doing well and expanding. Note names of people who might make good contacts. Sometimes you will find notices of people newly appointed to positions in charge of hiring. Also, read trade magazines and professional journals. If you do not subscribe, you may check them out at your local library.

Let me take a moment to say a few words about advertised openings. Be advised that it is a rare employer who knows exactly which applicant will best perform the work that needs to be done. It is your job to help the employer understand why you may be that person.

Ads consist of two main parts: job requirements (what the job requires you to do) and qualifications (what the employer surmises he or she may need from a candidate to get the job done). Before even considering the qualifications requested, study the job requirements and ask yourself, "Can I do this job? Could I perform well at such a position?" If the answer is no, then do not bother pursuing it. But if you can honestly answer yes, and if you would like to give the job a try, or at least learn more about it, then study the list of preferred qualifications. If your particular blend of talents and credentials is not a perfect match with the employer's best guess at qualifications, then make it your task to persuade the employer, just as you yourself are convinced, how your talents and knowledge equip you to excel at the position. Use Exercise 16 below to walk through this thinking process and to get a handle on responding to classified ads.

Exercise 16: Reviewing Classified Ads

Paste the classified ad that interests you in the left-hand column. Read the ad, and pull out any items that pertain to job requirements. List them under the Job Requirements column. Address each item with how you may be uniquely equipped to perform the function, writing your ideas in the next column under "Can I do this job?" Once you have satisfied yourself that you can do this job, read the ad again for desired qualifications. List these in the second column under "Qualifications." Finally, note how you can meet those qualifications—not entirely literally, but with an eye to the noted job requirements.

Classified Ad	Job Requirements	Can I do this job?
	1.	1.
	2.	2.
	3.	3.
	4.	4.
	Qualifications	How do I measure up?
	1.	1.
	2.	2.
	3.	3.
	4.	4.

Classified Ad	Job Requirements	Can I do this job?
	1.	1.
	2.	2.
	3.	3.
	4.	4.
	Qualifications	How do I measure up?
	1.	1.
	2.	2.
	3.	3.
	4.	4.

Classified Ad	Job Requirements	Can I do this job?
	1.	1.
	2.	2.
	3.	3.
	4.	4.
	Qualifications	How do I measure up?
	1.	1.
	2.	2.
	3.	3.
	4.	4.

Figure 23. Classified ad analysis

Let's look at an example (below). See how the responses in the final column realistically and creatively examine just what it takes to do this job.

Classified Ad	Job Requirements	Can I do this job?
Wanted: Employment Specialist Coordinate summer jobs program for inner city youth. Develop network of companies hiring. Coordinate advisory board. Teach job-seeking skills. Supervise interns. B.A. in vocational rehab and 1-3 yrs supervisory exp. M.A. preferred. Must have own transportation. Call (xxx) xxx-xxxx.	1. Program coord. skills (good communication well organized...) 2. Sales skills (w/employers) 3. Knowledge of job search skills (and teaching) 4. Supervisory skills.	1. Yes! I speak/write well; organized; Held offices in clubs. 2. Yes! Top cookie sales @ Girl scouts. 3. Yes! Interned @ rehab office in college. 4. Yes! Leader, pull my weight, inspire + motivate others. Experienced!
	Qualifications	How do I measure up?
	1. B.A. (M.A. preferred) in V.Rehab 2. Car 3. 1-3 yrs supervisory exp. 4.	1. B.A. (Anthropology). Related classes. Quick learner, people skills. 2. Easy! 3. Supervised/trained 8 whitpersons (1 yr); enthusiastic! 4.

Once you have completed the worksheet, as in any task in which you want to promote a product (in this case, yourself), take some time to anticipate possible objections and prepare responses. Then practice, and when you are ready, take your pitch to the employer. You will find more tips related to contacting and interviewing employers in the next chapter.

As you research and acquire leads, decide how best to pursue them. Begin with what you can do today to support your movement to a more meaningful and well-matched career. Write the daily tasks that you set for yourself into your calendar/planner, and then act.

Follow up frequently. Results will come from narrowing your field and from persistently focusing on and putting more energy into fewer, better leads and developing relationships with people as you pursue those leads. You will find the approach more fruitful than tossing your résumé around like confetti and hoping it will land in front of someone who will notice it and set out to court you. Quality over quantity is the name of the game.

MUSTERING COURAGE TO FOLLOW BLISS

Don't die with your music still in you.
—Oliver Wendell Holmes

After getting prepared, with all your materials in hand (résumé, portfolio, goals, contact lists, and leads), the time comes to act. For most, this is the scary part. This is, in a word, where the rubber meets the road. But this stage does not have to be a dreaded stage. It can—and should—offer joys of its own.

Using the Telephone

A woman stares out her kitchen window, periodically glancing first at the clock ticking dangerously close to 5:00 p.m., and then back at the phone perched on the counter. It seems to taunt her. Finally, she ushers her tense body to sit before the cold, impersonal phone. Time passes. She refuses to let herself answer those pleas to turn on the television, fold the laundry, and get supper started. No, she will make this call if it kills her. Suddenly, she surrenders and watches in panic as her fingers obey her and tap in the number. "Please don't answer. Please don't answer," she begs in a small voice.

"Management Associates."

She takes a deep breath. "I'd like to speak with personnel, please."

"May I ask what this is regarding?"

"Uh, yes. I saw your ad in the paper—you have a job?"

"I'm sorry, ma'am. We're only accepting résumés at this time. No calls."

The phone is back on the counter, and the woman's face falls into her hands. She has done it. She can tell her friends, her counselor, herself. She tried and no longer has to carry the guilt. But she is still preoccupied with a deep sense of failure.

The scene described above is not a lesson on how to do or not do a cold call. It is included as an appeal to common sense that screams out, "Why should anyone subject herself to this kind of torture?"

Just as I urge people to follow bliss, I also encourage them to stay within a reasonable level of comfort. Call when you feel jazzed about calling. Remember our fictional story about Nora, who dug herself into a hole trying to become more assertive, only to find that her assertiveness grew from her immersion in the things she loved? After making the list of "everyone you know," which we discussed in the previous chapter, begin making contacts—but begin where you feel most at home and most comfortable. Introductions will naturally branch out from there, and you will be much more effective in your contacts and less likely to procrastinate when you feel self-assured and confident.

That said, it is certainly true that the telephone is a direct, personal, and efficient way to contact a company. But many of us are intimidated by the phone and underutilize it. This has become increasingly true with our growing dependence upon emails and texting as a primary form of communication.

A prevalent fear I have heard is, "Won't I seem pushy?" Remember, it is not whether you call that makes you "pushy," it is how you handle the call. If you are a sensitive and courteous caller, people will appreciate your show of interest and in many cases will be more than happy to answer your questions. I emphasize five rules for effective phone use.

1. Be prepared.
2. Be somebody.
3. Be courteous.
4. Do not hang up empty-handed; articulate a next step.
5. Follow up.

Be Prepared

Locate a quiet and private space before you make your call so that you will not be interrupted and so that the person you are calling will be able to hear you. Keep in mind that putting someone on speaker generally worsens the quality of your voice.

Know why you are calling and what you want to say before you pick up the phone. Make a brief, confident presentation that does not unnecessarily burden the recipient of the call. If you feel a need to call but have no idea what to say, do not bother calling until you have figured that out. Otherwise, you will waste the other person's time as well as your own. (This may be a useful rule of thumb in your personal life as well!)

You may find a script helpful, so I have included a sample one below. Incorporate your own words so it reads more naturally. If you do not like using a script, then at least jot down questions you wish to ask and the things you want to be sure to cover. Keep a pen and paper handy to take down the information. Do not count on your memory! What if someone gives you a fifteen-letter, unusual name or a lengthy address? You will also need to be prepared to respond to questions about yourself. Have a résumé handy and perhaps some notes about how you might answer key questions.

Exercise 17: Sample Phone Script

The following script covers most items you will want to include in a job-related telephone call. Fill in the blanks in a way that makes sense for you, or read through and prepare an original script that fits you best.

Good morning. This is _____, calling for _____.
Is (Mr./Ms./Dr.) _____ available? …

Hello, (Mr./Ms./Dr.) _____. This is _____ [name], and I learned from _____[lead source] that you are currently looking to add some people to your field office in _____ [location]. Do you have two or three minutes to chat?

[If "No"] Fine. When would be a good time to call back?

[If "Yes"] Great! I was excited to hear of your expansion. I'm familiar with your agency, and I have been impressed with your company mission. Could you tell me if you have prepared a schedule for conducting interviews? I would love to come in and talk with you about your needs and what I can offer. When would be the best time for you? [You may need to respond to questions here about your qualifications. But do not waste the person's time if you are not asked; that can be covered during the interview.]

Where are you located?

Thank you for your time. I really look forward to seeing you next Thursday. What materials would you like me to bring?

Okay. I will see you on Thursday at 3:00 p.m. at your office. Thank you again!

Be Somebody

Do not say, "I am calling to find out about job openings." Instead, try something like, "Hi, this is Joe Somebody calling for Mary Employer. Is Ms. Employer available?" Or perhaps, "This is Joe Somebody calling. Larry Coverletter suggested I give the clinical director a call. Could you give me the name and correct spelling of the director's name? Ida Boss? Thank you. Is Ms. Boss in?" With the latter statement, you will run a much lower risk of being "screened out" and will sound much more confident and in control.

Be Courteous

Show your appreciation for every piece of information (as you write it down) and for the help you receive, from the front desk receptionist on up. (The receptionist may be the most powerful individual in the firm! Know his or her name, too.) Being courteous, by the way, does not mean immediately agreeing to hang up so that you can wait for hours for a return call. You can be courteous, kind, and assertive at the same time. Try an approach like this: "I know that Ms. Boss is very busy; I may be difficult to reach, and I do not want her to waste a call. Can you give me some times when I might try to call her back?" Then, be sure you follow up when you say you will.

Articulate the Next Step

The next step may be as simple as getting the person to agree to your sending a résumé in the mail. Who is going to refuse that? There is a continuum of things you may get from a phone call. Try for high on the list if you dare. (You may have to trust your gut on this.) Then, work your way down. Ask for

- a job offer (a rare occurrence, but you never know),
- a job interview,
- an opportunity to check back later regarding openings,
- another job lead or contact, or
- an opportunity to send a résumé or other material.

Follow Up

If the employer suggests that you call back in three weeks or six months, write a note to yourself immediately, place the note in your calendar, and follow through as promised. Send materials you have promised right away, and then follow up with a phone call to ensure it has been received. Thank-you notes always give you an edge, even if only to thank someone for taking a few minutes to speak with you. (I am amazed at how rare this simple gesture remains.) In a thank-you note, you can emphasize things you want to be remembered for and add any pertinent details about yourself that you neglected to mention or want to include.

Interviewing

Most interview questions serve not only to gather information on skills and qualifications but also to reveal the applicant's values, attributes, and working style. Many applicants, however, make the mistake of only responding to questions literally, providing facts but perhaps missing opportunities to respond fully to the employer's need to get to know the person behind the information. I do not need to tell you the facts about yourself and your qualifications;

however, I can help to demystify some commonly asked interview questions by exploring what employers really want to know when they pose them.

1. "Tell me about yourself."

This one stumps a lot of people, some because they have not done the exhaustive work of really getting to know themselves; others because it seems like such a huge question, and they are not sure what to emphasize. Here the employer seems to be asking for personal data. In fact, embarking on a personal story or a laundry list of qualities unrelated to the job at hand is not the way to respond to this one. Instead, share special interests or hobbies that can illustrate your suitability to the position, company, or milieu in question. For example, tell how you have established quick rapport with people through your ham radio hobby or how you used your creative talents in designing your own clothes. Let your personality shine through.

2. "Have you ever done this kind of work before?"

The interviewer in this instance really wants to know how quickly you will be up and running in the job. "Yes" would be a literal response, but it is not enough. Briefly tell when and where you have done similar work, and add what you enjoyed about it or highlight a specific achievement. If the literal answer is "no," do not stop there either. Share some experience that was similar in some way, or at the very least mention your ability to learn quickly.

3. "Why do you want to work here?"

In other words, "What is your motivation?" or "What can you tell me that I would enjoy hearing with regard to how wonderful we are?" The employer may be asking either or both. Convey your enthusiasm for the position, honestly and with your own personal style. Do not answer why you want a job, but why you want *this* job. (For example, perhaps you want to expand your skills, you are attracted to the company's reputation for excellent training, or you're wild about widgets.)

4. "Why did you leave your last job?"

Here the interviewer wants reassurance. Are you going to repeat an unwanted action—quit or perform poorly so the employer will have to fire you? Whatever happened and however horrible, reassure the employer through your self-assured manner that you will not be a troublemaker. Answer honestly, but be brief, and include how you have since fixed the problem, if there was a problem. Do not go into a long-winded debate, and do not speak in an angry, ungrateful, or dismissive way about your former employer. Do not try to convince the interviewer of your rightness and the former employer's wrongness. That tactic will burden the employer with unnecessary details and may cause her to see you as a victim, or worse as a problem, not in control of your own behavior. A blaming tone also uses up valuable interview time better spent talking about your assets. Take the higher road.

I have spent a fair amount of time interviewing people for jobs. I remember well one person who came to me, about whom I had heard rumors of "poor boundaries" in her previous position. I was not nearly as concerned about what may have happened in that previous job as I was interested in where she had landed. I asked her very directly about the reason for leaving her last job. She presented as evasive and unwilling to talk about it. She did not get the job, but before we ended the interview, I encouraged her to think about that question. I would be willing to interview her in the future if she could persuade me that she had effectively addressed the issue. Several months later, she returned, and I had an opportunity to ask the same question. This time, she went into a brief but illuminating description of the actions she had taken to work through underlying issues related to a former work relationship. She demonstrated ownership of her responsibility in the matter and persuaded me that she had grown through the experience. That was good enough for me. She turned out to be one of the highest-performing employees I ever hired.

5. "What are your salary requirements?"

Of course, the interviewer wants to know that he can afford to hire you, but he may be asking this question for other reasons. Perhaps it is a new position, and he lacks information about the usual salaries for this line of work. Or perhaps he wants to know how low you will go as you begin to negotiate. At this point, you will want to put the ball back into the interviewer's court by asking for the salary range. You may then choose a figure within that range in a place that seems fair and reasonable to you, given your perceived worth. You may choose to go a little high, but if that is the case show that you are open to negotiate. If the interviewer will not give you a range, then you name a range and negotiate from there. You may want to factor in the potential for advancement in this setting, and this may be a good time to ask about that; namely, about merit increases and the annual performance review process. Whatever you do, know ahead of time your absolute minimum needs, and do not settle for less.

I once found myself in a position of making a change from a high-paying career to one that typically paid much less. I knew that I would likely need to take a pay cut, but for me it was a quality of life issue, and I decided I would be willing to take a $20K pay cut. Nevertheless, I did not have much experience in the new field I was looking at, and as an entry-level employee, I worried that the salary offered may still fall below the amount at which I had arrived. Near the end of my interview, I did receive an offer—and as feared, it came in about $10K less than my established low point. Without dragging anything out, I calmly and clearly stated to the interviewer my gratitude for the time she had taken with me and my apologies that I had already decided upon the lowest point I was able to go. I shared that number with her—and promptly excused myself, fully expecting this was the end of my road. That was on a Friday afternoon. At about eight o'clock on Monday morning, I received a call that the employer was willing to meet my salary requirement. The lesson? Everything is negotiable.

6. "Describe your greatest strengths."

Here the interviewer will learn not only what you can do but also how you feel about yourself and how confidently and honestly you can present yourself. Share qualities that are most relevant to the job in question. Tooting our own horns does not come naturally to most of us, but practice makes perfect. Practice with your friends a few times before the interview. Get their feedback too; often others see our finest qualities much more readily than we see our own.

7. "Tell me about your greatest weaknesses."

The interviewer here is really asking the same thing as in the previous question, but from the other side. After all, our greatest strengths are also are greatest weaknesses, just viewed from another angle. Understand that weaknesses provide clues to dominant qualities, which usually serve you somehow. Be honest, and do not apologize for who you are. Show how you accommodate for perceived weaknesses. Instead of saying, "My coworkers are always telling me I am rude and detached," you might say instead, "I sometimes get so absorbed in my work that I lose touch with the people around me, and I can appear disengaged. This means I get a lot done [strength], but I do need to make a point of checking in with the people on my team to make sure I am maintaining strong working relationships [accommodation]."

8. "What would your previous supervisors or coworkers say about you?"

This is another way of getting at your dominant qualities. You can prepare for this question ahead of time by actually asking this question of your previous supervisors and coworkers and reviewing your letters of recommendation. It is a good question, because you can honestly respond to it and describe yourself in a highly favorable way without feeling unnecessarily embarrassed. After all, this is what others say about you, not what you say about yourself, so you are not really bragging. But do be sure you can back up what you are saying.

9. "Do you have your own transportation?"

Here the interviewer wants reassurance that you will be able to get to your place of employment reliably and on time. Whether or not you have a reliable car, be ready to convey that "you've got this"; have a plan or solution in mind, and be ready to share it. Even if you do have a car, in addition to a simple yes, it would not hurt to add that you have a strong work ethic and can assure the interviewer that you will be reliable—if that's an honest answer! (And I hope it is.) That response addresses the underlying concern directly.

10. "Do you have any health problems I need to know about?"

You are required by law to answer only as it pertains to the job requirements. There is no need to share information that is not relevant to the job. If you have seizures that are well controlled with medication, for example, share this information only if your own personality demands it; that is, share it only if you will be so tied up in knots for hiding it that you will not be able to perform well and may even find your condition exacerbated. What the employer really wants to know here is whether you are dependable or if she should expect a lot of absences. Do tell if you have a medical condition that restricts you from performing the job in some way, and then suggest an accommodation or a few options if possible. For example, if flashing lights give you migraine headaches, can your phone be altered? If you have a disability or health concern that you feel could generate some issues one way or another on the job, read up on the Americans with Disabilities Act (ADA) or see a vocational rehabilitation counselor who can better inform or advocate for you.

11. "Where do you see yourself in five years?"

Here the interviewer may be wondering how ambitious you are, and your answer could be received in a couple of different ways. The employer may seek someone who will stay in place at the position of hire and remain there for a long time without becoming dissatisfied. Another employer may like a person with more ambition, someone with lofty career goals, ready to climb the corporate ladder. If you are perceived as someone with ambition who may end up leaving the company in question for another position, that could be seen as a bad thing or a good thing. Some employers are sincere in their wishes for employees to thrive and grow no matter where it takes them. The most important thing here is to be honest. Do not try to present yourself as other than who you are, and you will be far more likely to be accepted in the place that will be the best fit for you.

12. "Do you have any questions for me?"

Here, the interviewer appears to be letting you ask about anything he may have omitted. Chances are this question comes at the end of the interview. Be brief but memorable. Some questions that can elicit valuable information for you include the following. (Choose only one or two, unless you have a lot of time remaining.)

- What might a typical day look like for me here?
- What would you say is required for someone to excel in this position?
- How did the position come to be open?
- With whom would I be working?
- Who would be my supervisor? Can you describe your supervisory style?
- How did you come to work here? What do you like about working here?
- May I see where I would be working?
- What's the next step in the application process? (What more do you need from me; when will I hear from you; may I call you back; etc.)

Some questions may be specific to your particular field or area of expertise. A schoolteacher, for example, may want to know if essential supplies are provided by the employer. A salesperson may want to know if sales leads will be provided and how much pay may be based on commission.

Volunteer and Internship Opportunities

If your path to the job of your dreams requires a bit more experience than you can readily access, you might be a good candidate for an unpaid internship or volunteer position. In most cases, such experiences are built into educational or training programs and limited to a certain number of required hours—generally six or nine months, give or take, depending on the program. Although such arrangements are unpaid, they can provide valuable experience and a chance to demonstrate your ability. Nevertheless, you will still need to apply and be accepted into such a position. The application process pretty much mirrors what you need to do in a job search.

One word of caution: Keep in mind that internship and practicum experiences are intended to provide learning experiences, and as such there is generally not an expectation that you would come into the position with work-ready skills. The understanding is that you will develop these through the internship experience. Some internship sites are better than others at holding to this principle. Make sure you are selective in choosing a supervisor from whom you think you could learn what you need to learn, someone who will be relatable and accessible to you.

Overcoming Self-Sabotage

I have felt compelled to follow my bliss for much of my life, but it has not been easy. I recall moments when my greatest enemy has indeed been my own self-doubt, when I have chickened out instead of moving forward. No matter how clearly I knew what needed to be done, that nasty little voice of self-sabotage taunted me. "You're dreaming! Get real! You haven't got a chance!" And I listened. Many of us know that voice that admonishes, "You shouldn't. You don't deserve it"; or the one that insists, "You can't. You're not good enough."

You should. You can. You must.

Let me share the story of someone with enormous strength of spirit who was able to find great success in life and work in spite of the fact that hardly anyone else believed in him—and some might argue, justifiably so.

A young man I'll call Fred walked into a last-stop career placement office one day after meeting with one rejection after another. My colleague described him as a young man who had an infectious smile, a clear sense of purpose, and some clear cognitive limitations. (He bore the label "intellectual disability.")

Fred had been to several public agencies requesting assistance, each time insisting that he wanted to be a doctor. Repeatedly, he met with varying degrees of incredulity and disparagement, and in the end encouragement to take a fast-food or housekeeping job. To his credit, he kept going until he found my friend Bernie.

Bernie and I worked in the same program, the Training and Placement Service (TAPS) of the Epilepsy Foundation of America. We were accustomed to stories like Fred's. We had both been surprised enough times by people to learn never to second-guess them. Our approach was to meet the person where he was, trust in the wisdom of the person's dreams, and support him however we could.

Without attempting to discourage Fred, Bernie openly discussed the educational challenges he faced. He explained that doctors required many years of education and suggested he might want to begin by getting his high school diploma. Fred was excited. He signed up for a GED program. Bernie also learned that Fred did not know much about the health-care industry, and together he and Fred explored ways to learn more about it. Fred decided to volunteer as a candy striper at a local hospital, just to get the lay of the land.

Through his volunteer work, one day Fred learned of a job opening for an orderly at the hospital. He applied for the job, and because of the good reputation he had built up as a volunteer, the staff were thrilled to hire him.

The next time Bernie saw Fred, he showed up at the TAPS office dressed in a white orderly jacket, glowing, as he proudly announced, "I'm a doctor!"

Fred believed in his dream, and with persistence, he realized it. In this case, one might say that he had been naming it incorrectly; but this can be the way of bliss. It can work in mysterious ways for all of us. It may not be clear for a long time where our hearts are leading us, but if we simply trust the process, it will not fail us. There may be a job just over the horizon that you cannot name, because it is just as much a mystery to you as being an orderly was to Fred. Fred followed the star nearest to him, and it led him right where he belonged.

Trust the process. I have heard the phrase many times, and it remains a useful reminder. Give yourself time and room to stumble. Surround yourself with people who believe in you and can support you in your process.

Remember too that change can be painful, no matter how right, because it is always accompanied by loss. This brings up the paradox that exists in following bliss. It may be tempting to assume that the task of following bliss is an indulgent and always pleasing one, requiring little effort. On the contrary, it can be a most agonizing endeavor.

I recall as a young person listening to a sermon in a small-town Catholic church. The priest was a guest speaker—a young, handsome fellow invited to inspire the young people in the parish to consider a religious vocation. I am sure the elders of the congregation viewed his rough language and approach as somewhat unseemly, but his message reached me in a powerful way. He told the story of his own calling, characterizing himself as a typical young person whose first response to the blessed event was a vehement, "Oh, shit!" It was not a groundless gut reaction. He knew that he would face many sacrifices and demands should he follow the call, but he also knew that he could not fulfill his purpose in any other way.

The moments of ecstasy that accompany the fulfillment of a clear sense of purpose are routinely balanced with moments of agony. Both contribute to the richness in life and ensure our active participation here on earth.

On the other hand, work is not meant to equal drudgery. Work is what we do, and it ought to bring us joy. Moreover, choosing work that feeds our soul is no luxury—it is a responsibility. If you have a gift lying dormant because you feel that using it would somehow be "cheating" at life, think again. You may be committing a great injustice not only to yourself but also to your community and the world.

Suppose you know all of this. You get it. You know what needs to be done, but you still cannot seem to do the right thing. You are sabotaging your own success.

Of all the demographic segments of the population we might point to as having the least promise of ever finding and keeping meaningful and satisfying employment, one stands head and shoulders above the rest: the discouraged worker. Discouraged people find ways to sabotage their success every step of the way. The one thing I believe discouraged people lack most, once again, is imagination.

The surest way out of a rut is to see things differently and to see different things. As we have heard many times, we need to learn to see the other side, the silver lining, the rest of the picture. This simply requires imagination, and any exercise that stretches imagination can help here. (See exercise 1, "Point A to Point B," in this text.)

You can use this essential faculty, imagination, to work out any obstacle on your career path. Perhaps at first glance, your resistance to picking up that phone looks like mere laziness. Can you imagine what else might be entering the equation? It may seem that a prospective employer "just doesn't like me." What else may be part of this picture? Joining forces with a group of others enables a creative collaboration that can produce even more imaginative responses than you can produce on your own.

Often it takes an enormous amount of imagination to follow bliss, but it insists upon our attention. What is it telling you now, asking of you? Take your questions to a lump of clay or an original fairy tale. Imagination thrives in places like these, and a peer, art therapist, or expressive arts therapist can be an invaluable partner in helping you to discover and learn from the rich images that live there.

Sometimes self-sabotage results from deep-seated feelings of being undeserving, or put another way, an inability to imagine ourselves as deserving persons. We may know intellectually that *everyone* deserves happiness and fulfillment, but on an emotional level, this can be excruciatingly difficult to imagine or accept. I appeal to people's sense of responsibility in these cases. Do not do it because you want to or because it feels good; do it because it is your work. It is your responsibility. You are called. Do not short-change the world. Change the world!

Some people simply cannot tolerate change easily. The first step to overcoming this obstacle is to recognize it for what it is. Once you understand the nature of the problem and admit to it, you can put it outside of yourself and work with it. Take risks in small steps. Remember too that routine is a good thing. Do not just cast routine into the wind; build new routines to replace the old. Eventually they will become familiar and comforting, too.

> *The surest way out of a rut is to see things differently and to see different things.*

Another example of self-sabotage sounds like this: "I couldn't take that job. It's so wonderful. I'm sure someone else wants it/deserves it/could excel at it more than I." Would we really give our bliss away? Some people would. But the truth is, these fantasies about other people are rarely, if ever, true. Everyone's bliss is a little different. Not everyone wants to be president of the United States—believe me! Many of us may want to be able to tell a president what to do, but that is not the same as actually doing the job of a president. Not everyone possesses a passion to be a rock star either.

I remember working to establish some career goals with a young woman who had an intellectual disability. Do you know what her deepest, most secret dream was? To have an apartment of her own. As an outsider, I could see that the goal may require some planning and work, but it was absolutely within her reach. We are all provided with the tools and strength we require to succeed, and never are we called to a purpose beyond the reach of our abilities.

Finding an Image of Strength

There is a simple method I use to rise out of states of vulnerability and discouragement. I sit with the ill feelings and let an image emerge; then I work with the image so that I may better appreciate its complexity and how it serves me. By "working with the image," I am referring to rendering it in a drawing, sculpture, story, song, or some other art modality.

I recall one of the first times I used this exercise. I was teaching a class of first-year graduate students in expressive arts therapy. It was about two months into the semester, about the time when, as typically happens with group dynamics, the honeymoon was over. This can be a painful time of learning for anyone who facilitates groups, and as I was a relative novice on the faculty, it was painful for me. In short, I had not met the expectations of some of my students. As a core faculty of expressive arts therapy, I was an art and music therapist but not a skilled psychodramatist, and I could not accommodate for what some of those students perceived as an inadequacy. The students realized I was not their perfect teacher. In their minds, I had failed them.

At the time, I was preparing to teach an intensive weekend class. I decided to try working with the image of weakness that loomed before me so large, to see if that would lead me to a different image, preferably one of strength, one with which I could arm myself before the next class.

The image of weakness that came to me was that of an organic sponge. It fit my style of facing conflict to a T. I regarded the sponge and thought, *Yes, this is me. I do not deflect like a shield nor do I attack like a sword. Rather, I soak in criticisms with every fiber of my being. It is pure agony. The soaking process is not paralyzing, but it does require pause and takes a lot of time. I absorb every accusation, every glance, every word, every insult, fully and completely. I slow down.* Staying with the image, I considered, *But I am never destroyed, and I never lose the integrity of my shape. A sponge is malleable, flexible. It can be manipulated, influenced—but a sponge is not clay. The impressions cannot force me into something I am not.*

And so, the very same image I felt described my weakness became my image of strength as well. The exercise rejuvenated me, and I was able to conclude that intensive weekend class having gained a new level of respect from the students. It may seem a bit of a mystery how I gained that respect, since I did not earn in one day that credential they initially felt they required of me. I expect the change had more to do with the way I carried myself and presented myself—just as I was.

Images of self-sabotage must be dealt with again and again in our lives, for they tend to recur. The better acquainted we become with imagination, the easier the way through. Other people, particularly expressive arts therapists and personal coaches, can be particularly helpful in identifying blocks to success that may be difficult to see and navigating through—and past—maladaptive patterns and back on the road to bliss.

CLOSING REMARKS

It's your road, and yours alone.
Others may walk it with you,
But no one can walk it for you.
—Rumi

In the preceding pages, I have tried to walk you through a process of reflection, self-inventorying, and career-life planning. Along the way, I have challenged some popular career-counseling methodologies and offered a perspective shaped by my approach to the practice of career-life planning as an art and a spiritual quest.

My goal has been to update, simplify, and demystify the process of career-life planning and to challenge and inspire you. But more than anything else, I hope I have managed to ignite your imagination and bolster your courage a bit. I hope also that I have conveyed my personal faith in all people and their diverse talents, as well as my belief that when it comes to career niches, there are no hopeless cases.

My final counsel to you is simple: when you become confused along the way of your career path, when you wonder which direction to take, let yourself be guided by the wisdom that judges the rightness of a thing—a decision, choice, or act—by the magnitude of passion or excitement that accompanies it.

Let your own imagination be inspired, and muster the courage to follow your bliss. They have not yet failed me, and I trust they will not fail you.

CREATING WITH THE WORKPLACE: FOREWORD TO THE 2000 EDITION

Experience teaches that the great frontiers for the creative process are places where it is least recognized. Today the workplace is that unexplored region of creative discovery and practice. Both leaders and workers know that something has to change.

There is a great reservoir of creative potential that needs to be released, but we have yet to find the way. Well-intentioned efforts to introduce the creative imagination into the workplace tend to be characterized by superficial outcomes, such as short-lived trends of poets reading to corporate boards who feel the need for something outside the lines of work as usual. In an effort to inspire and retain talented employees, creativity consultants redesign work environments and make them more spacious, illuminated by natural light, and open to the natural world. All of these efforts are important steps toward a deeper experience of reality, but the technician mentality that drives the workplace today is simply incapable of contacting the undiscovered resources of the creative imagination that lie waiting in individuals, groups, and places.

As I was preparing a lecture on creativity and workplace, my fourteen-year-old daughter said, "Daddy, those are two words that people don't usually connect to one another." My daughter is absolutely correct. Creativity is something we do, if we have the time, outside work. We imagine retirement as a period when we can focus on what we really want to do with our lives and then discover that we miss the connections to people, situations, and problems that provide the interactive fuels of creation. The creative imagination is an intelligence that operates outside the lines, and the workplace is the ultimate arena for linear thought and action.

During the seventeenth, eighteenth, and early nineteenth centuries, English and German thinkers defined the imagination as an intermediate realm that integrates rational, intuitive, and sensory knowing. The creative imagination draws together the resources of a person's different faculties and generates new things based on a transformative mix of often-unlikely elements. Everything from experience, good and bad, contributes to the outcomes that lie outside the parameters of linear cause and effect. Imagination makes leaps into new ways of perceiving and engaging the world that can be likened to the discoveries of late twentieth-century physics.

The workplace of today has not been significantly influenced by the discoveries of the new physics. It is a realm shaped largely by the old linear science of creative imagination. For two centuries, the science of work has stayed strictly within the lines. Imagination is commonly defined as unreality, and imaginative people are viewed as escaping from the real world.

We all need our retreats from the world of work to regenerate and refocus our creative energies. There are many pathogens in the workplace in terms of stress, fear, and monotony. My experience constantly indicates that the things that oppress us the most carry the seeds of major transformations of consciousness. I realize that I need the community of people within the workplace and our collaborative efforts toward shared goals to keep me connected to the real stuff of life. I create together with the world and not completely apart from it. Work and daily life offer the stuff of creative imagination and especially the irritants and problems that push the creative process into new frontiers of engagement.

As the human resources director at my workplace said to me, "Creativity is very hard to cultivate in the workplace and very easy to destroy." She went on to describe how fear is the primary threat to creative expression at work. What happens if I take a risk and it goes against the grain of workplace values? What will I do if I lose this job?

Creative imagination requires us to place things in new relationships and to go beyond the boundaries of how things are presently done, whereas the workplace typically requires the opposite from people. How can these contradictions be addressed? Is there hope for the practice of creative imagination in the workplace? Even though it may be widely recognized that creativity is good for the workplace, that it fosters greater productivity and invention, helps people to feel better about themselves and their jobs, and thoroughly energizes environments, it may be viewed as counter-culture, threatening the business. Companies and organizations are simply not set up to deliver the creative process. Too much creativity can actually get you into trouble within environments where you are expected to stay completely within the lines and meet standardized expectations.

There are many aspects of work that require strict adherence to rules and regulations and linear problem-solving. The practice of imagination in the workplace must ultimately work together with boundaries and concrete expectations. It is not a matter of embracing one without the other. Experience indicates that restrictions can often feed creation, as long as there is receptivity to divergent possibilities and new discoveries. Leadership needs to model respect for new ideas and make it safer for people to experiment and try something different.

Paradigm inconsistencies can evaporate immediately when we discover that something new works and offers great value. Therefore, the contradictions between imaginative and linear thinking are not insurmountable. I believe the ongoing separation between creativity and work results from a comprehensive inability to grasp what can be done differently. Simply stated, we know that the practice of creation can be good for the workplace, but we don't know how to do it. Superficial gimmicks will do more to undermine the practice of imagination and keep it outside organizational life.

I believe that it will be the efforts of inspired individuals that will bring about the integration of work and creative imagination. People guided by visions can change anything. As increasing numbers of people begin to share the same vision and work toward it together, it becomes a consensually validated reality. The primary force for change in the workplace will be the consciousness of workers who feel that something very important is lacking in their lives.

We typically say that the infusion of imagination into the workplace depends upon visionary leaders who establish and hold the space for others to create. The role of leadership is crucial, but I believe that sweeping changes in organization life are more apt to occur through a rising tide of worker aspirations. When these positive shifts in consciousness occur, leadership manifests a responsive intelligence that helps the innovations take root and grow.

This book is one of these inspired and important individual contributions to a larger change in consciousness. The author knows that something is missing in the world, and she has taken action to do something different. Her book's title is based upon Joseph Campbell's exhortation to "Follow your bliss!" As John Lennon said, "imagine all the people" following their instincts about how to create a better and more complete life. I also have no doubt that more blissful experience at work will be more productive and good for the bottom line, but we still don't know how to go about doing this.

[Haley Fox] offers many practical steps toward realizing a more productive and creative relationship with work. This book reads both like a challenge and a common-sense course of action:

- Stretch the imagination and watch how it changes the realities that appear beyond our control.
- There is power in the practice of imagination that has yet to be tapped.
- Everything depends upon how we think about things.
- Pay attention to the things that bother you and actually "indulge" them, [Fox] says. See your problems as doorways to change. They are telling you what needs attention.
- Work can be a labor of the heart, the author says, and this power can be channeled in new ways.

In addition to giving a big picture of a new relationship to work, [Fox] offers many practical tips on résumé writing, job counseling, goal-setting, prioritizing, and so forth. Ultimately, it is the sustained application of the creative imagination to these ordinary things that really changes the world. The realization of a more creatively fulfilling workplace is based upon what [Fox] calls "intuitions of the future" and new possibilities of what we can do with organizational life.

[Haley Fox] is making her individual contribution to the rising tide of creativity in the workplace. Read this book and discover what you can do. Following your bliss is often difficult. Setbacks and disappointments are inevitably on the way to creating something new. The sense of bliss is the vision, the guide, and the affirmation that something different is possible. It is not just momentary pleasure. Bliss can be a beautiful idea of what can someday exist. Trust your "intuitions of the future" and be assured that the creative process can ultimately deliver you to a new place.

This book's focus on the workplace challenges us all to work together to re-vision and recreate the place that binds us all.

Shaun McNiff
2000

REFERENCES

Barlow, E. 1995. "Creating the Future: The Journey towards the Next Millennium." Paper presented at Mount Wachusett Community College, Gardner, MA, September 1995.

Bowman, M. 2016. "My Complete List of Career Assessments." http://www.marthabowman.info/my_complete_list.htm.

Burns, G. 1998. *Nature-Guided Therapy: Brief Integrative Strategies for Health and Well-Being.* Philadelphia: Brunner/Mazel.

Byrne, R. (2006). *The Secret.* New York: Beyond Words Publishing.

Cantwell, M. (2013). *Be a Free-Range Human: Escape the 9 to 5, Create a Life You Love and Still Pay the Bills.* Philadelphia, Pennsylvania: Kogan Page Ltd.

Campbell, J. (1988). *Joseph Campbell and the Power of Myth, with Bill Moyers.* Betsy Sue Flowers (Ed.). New York: Doubleday.

Chopra, D. (2014). "Living Carefree: A Meditation with Deepak Chopra." Retrieved from https://www.youtube.com/watch?v=XSNpGyG2jSw&app=desktop.

Clear, J. (2017, February 13). "Forget about Setting Goals. Focus on This Instead." Retrieved from http://jamesclear.com/goals-systems.

Coelho, P. (2014). *The Alchemist.* New York: Harper Collins.

Covey, S. (1989). *The Seven Habits of Highly Effective People.* New York: Simon & Schuster, Inc.

Csikszentmihalyi, M. (1990). *Flow: The Psychology of Optimal Experience.* New York: Harper and Row.

Dyer, W. (2014). *I Can See Clearly Now.* Carlsbad, California: Hay House, Inc.

Fields, J. & Nicodemus, R. (2014). *Everything That Remains: A Memoir by the Minimalists.* Asymmetrical Press.

Fox, H. (f.k.a. H. Barba) (1988). "Toward a Psychology of Recurring Imagery." Unpublished master's thesis, Lesley University.

Frick, D. (2009). *Implementing Servant-Leadership: Stories from the Field*. LaCrosse, Wisconsin: Viterbo University.

Hillman, J. (1977). *Re-visioning Psychology*. New York: Harper & Row.

Jeffers, S. (1987). *Feel the Fear and Do It Anyway*. New York: Harcourt Brace Janovich.

Keller-Dupree, B. (2016, September 24) "Creatively Using Joy in the Classroom, with B. Behrend." Roundtable discussion, Association for Creativity in Counseling biennial conference, Savannah, Georgia.

Knill, P., Fox, H. (f.k.a. H. Barba), Fuchs, M. (1995/2005). *Minstrels of Soul: Intermodal Expressive Therapy*. Toronto: Palmerston Press/EGS Press.

Kondo, M. (2014). *The Life-Changing Magic of Tidying Up: The Japanese Art of De-Cluttering*. Berkeley: Ten Speed Press.

Lanza, R. (2009). *Biocentrism: How Life and Consciousness Are the Keys to Understanding the True Nature of the Universe*. Dallas, Texas: BenBella Books, Inc.

McAuliffe, G. (1993, Winter). "Career as an Imaginative Quest." *American Counselor*, 13–36.

McCarthy, B. (Producer & Director). (1991). *Sam Keen: Your Mythic Journey, with Bill Moyers* [videotape]. New York: Public Affairs Television, Inc.

McNiff, S. (1988). *Fundamentals of Art Therapy*. Springfield, Illinois: Charles C. Thomas.

Ogburn, W. & Thomas, D. (Winter 2011–2012). "Are Inventions Inevitable? A Note on Social Evolution," *Political Science Quarterly*, 126 (4), pp. 83–98. Retrieved from http://www.jstor.org/stable/2142320.

Pimentel, R. & Lotito, M. (1992). *The Americans with Disabilities Act: Making the ADA Work for You*. Chatsworth, California: Milt Wright and Associates.

Reich, R. (2011). "The Truth about the Economy." Retrieved from https://www.youtube.com/watch?v=JTzMqm2TwgE

Reich, R. (1987). *Tales of a New America*. New York: Random House.

Robert Half (November 29, 2018). "10 Best Job Search Websites." Retrieved at: https://www. roberthalf.com/blog/job-market/10-best-job-search-websites on May 10, 2019.

Sanders, B. (2016). *Our Revolution*. New York: St. Martin's Press.

Siegel, B. (1986). *Love, Medicine, and Miracles*. New York: Harper & Row.

Thomas, T. (2016). *Who Do You Think You Are?* New York: Morgan James Publishing.

Wegmann, R., Chapman, R. & Johnson, M. (1989). *Work in the New Economy*. (Revised Ed.). Alexandria, Virginia: American Association for Counseling & Development and Indianapolis: JIST Works, Inc. (copublishers).

INDEX

action words, 111
art therapy, 22, 150, 179, 214, 216
bliss, 5, 11, 12, 69, 94
career assessment, 71, 215
catharsis, 56
cover letter, 122, 136, 143, 145
Covey, 168, 169, 170, 215
curriculum vita, 102
dominant qualities, 45, 47, 101, 104, 121, 153, 199
expressive arts therapy, 22, 31, 64, 210
Frick, Donald M., 5, 38, 216
goal-setting, 152, 155
guided imagery, 22, 96, 97, 101
Hillman, 23, 216
image, 36, 50, 73, 82, 84, 96, 104, 110, 123, 210, 211
imaginal realm, 22, 29
imagination, 7, 8, 9, 10, 11, 12, 23, 24, 25, 27, 29, 30, 34, 171, 173, 207, 208, 211, 213
informational interview, 146
intellect, 62, 71, 72, 82, 86
interview, 24, 71, 131, 134, 140
job interview, 193
Keen, 24, 216
Knill, 5, 101, 214, 216
leads, 20, 22, 27, 172, 173, 178, 179, 181, 183, 186, 187, 202
letters of recommendation, 102, 136, 139, 140, 141, 199
LinkedIn, 139, 176
McNiff, 5, 7, 13, 101, 216
meditation, 66, 69, 148, 156, 215
myth, 33, 34, 35, 215
objective, 23, 27, 104, 108, 122, 123
personality, 46, 48, 52, 63, 106, 127, 128, 132, 194, 200
planner, 166, 186

ABOUT THE AUTHOR

Helen Nienhaus Barba, 2000   Haley Fox, 2020

Haley Fox (formerly known as Helen Nienhaus Barba) is a board-certified art therapist, a board-certified music therapist, and a registered expressive arts therapist, licensed as a professional clinical counselor in Minnesota and Massachusetts and also certified as a clinical supervisor in art therapy (ATCS). She has her PhD in clinical psychology and currently teaches graduate students in counseling and art therapy at Adler University in Chicago, Illinois. Much of this book's contents emerged from material acquired within a full-service private career-life planning practice spanning many years. In her private practice, for more than thirty years, Dr. Fox has applied her skills as an artist-psychotherapist to help people work through anxiety, depression, and other issues related to identifying and fulfilling career/life goals. She has brought her thorough knowledge of the job-seeking process to help people from all walks of life navigate a way through the complex and ever-changing job-search terrain. A self-proclaimed "résumé artist," Dr. Fox also relies upon well-developed creative writing skills to help clients craft powerful individual portfolios so critical to the job-seeking process. Dr. Fox coauthored the text *Minstrels of Soul: Intermodal Expressive Therapy* with Paolo Knill and Margo Fuchs; that book was first published in 1993 (Palmerston Press), republished in 2005 (EGS Press), and translated into Mandarin in 2016. Dr. Fox continues to nurture special academic interests in art-based research, human sexuality, resonance, ancient artifacts, and archetypal psychology.

Printed in the United States
By Bookmasters